Competition Law in Uruguay

Competition Law in Uruguay

Fourth Edition

Hector Ferreira
Bernardo Porras

This book was originally published as a monograph in the International Encyclopaedia of Laws/Competition Law.

Founding Editor: Roger Blanpain
General Editor: Frank Hendrickx
Volume Editors: Francesco Denozza & Alberto Toffoletto

Wolters Kluwer

Published by:
Kluwer Law International B.V.
PO Box 316
2400 AH Alphen aan den Rijn
The Netherlands
E-mail: international-sales@wolterskluwer.com
Website: lrus.wolterskluwer.com

Sold and distributed in North, Central and South America by:
Wolters Kluwer Legal & Regulatory U.S.
7201 McKinney Circle
Frederick, MD 21704
United States of America
Email: customer.service@wolterskluwer.com

Sold and distributed in all other countries by:
Air Business Subscriptions
Rockwood House
Haywards Heath
West Sussex
RH16 3DH
United Kingdom
Email: international-customerservice@wolterskluwer.com

Printed on acid-free paper

ISBN 978-94-035-0711-8

e-Book: ISBN 978-94-035-0712-5
web-PDF: ISBN 978-94-035-0713-2

Printed in the United Kingdom.

The Authors

Professor Hector Ferreira (born 20 March 1977) studied Law and obtained his Juris Doctor (JD) at the Catholic University of Uruguay in 1999. In 2004, he obtained his degree in Comparative and International Law at the Academy of American and International Law, Dallas, Texas, and in 2008, he studied US and Comparative Law and obtained his LLM at the University of California, Davis.

In 2004, he was appointed as assistant professor of Commercial Law and in 2008 as professor at the School of Law of the Catholic University of Uruguay where he presently teaches Commercial Law and Antitrust Law.

In 2007, Hector Ferreira also became associate professor in Commercial Law at the faculty of the School of Law of the University of Uruguay.

During 2008 and 2009, he was Foreign Associate with Schinner & Shain, LLP, San Francisco, where he dealt with, among others, monopoly law in the United States.

Professor Ferreira has been a member of the Uruguayan Bar since 2000, of the International Bar since 2006, and of the American Bar since 2008. He is presently a partner with Hughes & Hughes, Montevideo.

He has published many articles, in Spanish and English, on trade practices, competition law, and commercial law, in publications from the United States, the UK, Argentina, and Uruguay.

Professor Bernardo Porras (born 28 October 1971) studied Law and obtained his JD at the University of Uruguay in 2000. In 2001, he obtained his degree in Comparative and International Law at the Academy of American and International Law, Dallas, Texas.

In 2000, he was appointed as assistant professor of Foundations of Uruguayan Law and in 2002 as associate professor at the faculty of administrative law at the School of Law of the University of Uruguay, where he presently teaches Administrative Law and Economic and Regulatory affairs in competition law.

The Authors

In 2004, Bernardo Porras published his first study on the relations between Antitrust Law and Telecommunications in Uruguay which became a landmark in the development of the Uruguayan Antitrust.

Since 2005, he has been teaching a programme for enterprisers and corporate managers on practical legal issues concerning Antitrust Law.

Professor Porras has been a member of the Uruguayan Bar since 2000. He is presently a partner with Hughes & Hughes, Montevideo.

He has published many articles in English and Spanish on regulatory law, competition law, and administrative law, in publications from the United States, the UK, and Uruguay.

Table of Contents

List of Abbreviations

ANTEL	Telecommunication State's Company
ANCEL	Mobile Phones State's Company
ANP	Harbour's Authority
FNC	Fabricas Nacionales de Cerveza S.A
HHI	Herfindahl-Hirschman Index
MERCOSUR	South American Economic Organization
M&A	Mergers & Acquisitions
OSE	Drinkable water State's Company
PLUNA	Former Uruguayan Airlines
S.Ct	US Supreme Court
TTBE	Transfer of Technology Block Exemption
UK	United Kingdom
URSEC	Communication Services' Authority
URSEA	Water Services' Authority
URSEA	Energy Authority
US	United States

List of Abbreviations

General Introduction

§1. GENERAL BACKGROUND OF THE COUNTRY

I. Geography and Historical Background

1. The Oriental Republic of Uruguay is a country located in south-eastern South America, the name of which derived from its geographic location which is to the east of the Uruguayan River. It borders on Brazil in the north (state of *Rio Grande do Sul*), Argentina in the west (province of *Entre Ríos*), the estuary of *Río de la Plata* in the south, and the Atlantic Ocean in the east. The only land border it has is with *Río Grande do Sul*, Brazil.

2. The capital city is Montevideo, with a population of 1.5 million, and founded by Bruno Mauricio de Zabala in 1726. The official language of Uruguay is Spanish.

3. Uruguay is, mainly, a flat country. Its highest peak is the Cathedral Hill, 514 metres in altitude. Uruguay has some islands in the Uruguayan River and the *Isla de Lobos* in the Atlantic.org.

4. Even though Uruguay is a small country as compared to its neighbours (mainly Brazil and Argentina), it is not small in comparison to economically developed countries such as Denmark and Switzerland.

5. Before the discovery of America and the European colonization of the current Uruguayan territory, the area was inhabited by the Charruas' Tribe, a small group of wild natives that is still today associated with the Uruguayan nation. The Spanish Kingdom arrived in the Uruguayan territory in 1516, and the former inhabitants of Uruguay fiercely fought against the invaders.

6. Between 1680 and 1683, while in dispute with Spain over this region, Portuguese settlers established several colonies near *Río de la Plata*, among others, possibly *Colonia del Sacramento*. This colony was the origin of the capital city of one of the departments of the current Uruguay (Colonia), well known for its tourist attractions.

7. Notwithstanding the foregoing, Montevideo was founded by Spain in 1726 as a military base to defend the Eastern Province of the *Virreinato del Río de la Plata* from Portuguese invasions. Without precious metals, Uruguayan territory was from the Spanish standpoint a zone for resistance against Portugal. However, its natural and deep harbour became important even from a commercial perspective and soon started to compete with the Buenos Aires harbour. Furthermore, the rapid development of livestock activity gave the territory one of its most important activities, which survives even today.

8. The rivalry between Spain and Portugal continued throughout the seventeenth century, ending with the definitive supremacy of Spain, which imposed its Authority in the region through the so-called *Virreinato del Río de la Plata.*

9. Between 1810 and 1811, led by General José Gervasio Artigas, Uruguayan revolutionaries joined patriots from Buenos Aires against the Spanish Kingdom. Spanish authorities were driven out of Montevideo in 1814, and a national government was formed in 1815.

10. The Empire of Brazil took advantage of the above-mentioned situation and decided to invade the Uruguayan territory which had been conquered in 1821 and named *ProvinciaCisplatina*. However, a group of patriots led by General Juan Antonio Lavalleja claimed the Uruguayan territory by fighting against the Brazilians for two years. Finally, they declared Uruguay's independence in 1825. This declaration was internationally recognized in 1828 with the explicit support of the United Kingdom (UK).

11. Uruguay, as a free country, was politically organized as a Democratic Republic with a Unitarian State formed by nineteen departments (similar to states in a Federal regime) with Montevideo as the capital city. The country issued its Constitution in 1830, and General Fructuoso Rivera was sworn in as the first constitutional President of Uruguay.

12. In 1839, a civil war was declared between Rivera's supporters and the supporters of General Oribe (the second constitutional President of Uruguay). The civil war (known as *Guerra Grande*) lasted until 1851 and consolidated the two historical political parties of Uruguay; on the one hand the *Partido Colorado* – Red Party – (Rivera's supporters) and on the other hand the *Partido Blanco* – White Party – (Oribe's supporters). The said names were chosen on the basis of the colours of their respective flags.

13. Those colours are, until today, the emblems of the two traditional parties of Uruguay which, alternatively, led the country until 2005 when *FrenteAmplio* won the elections and its candidate Dr Tabaré Vazquez Rosa became the new President. The same political party formed the government after the 2009 elections when Mr José MujicaCordano won the elections in a second round against the White Party's candidate and former President, Dr Luis Alberto Lacalle. *FrenteAmplio* is a left-wing political party, formed mainly by dissident members of the traditional parties and independents after the last Uruguayan dictatorship (which lasted from 1973 to 1985).

14. Before the *FrenteAmplio* party won the elections in 2004, the Colorado Party had formed the government for almost the whole of the twentieth century. The only elections which the White Party won, and then consequently governed the country, were those held in 1958 and 1989.

15. In general, from 1865 to 1958, the Colorado Party continued to form the government and one of its most remarkable representatives, José Batlle y Ordoñez, led the country in two different periods (beginning in 1903 and in 1915). President Batlle y Ordoñez's administration is recognized as the most important landmark in Uruguayan history. During his presidency, relevant social and economic measures were implemented, and Uruguay was internationally recognized as a progressive country in Latin America.

16. As has been said, the White Party won the elections in 1958 and formed the government until 1966, when the Colorado Party won the elections again. The elected President, Mr Oscar Daniel Gestido, passed away during his presidency, and the Vice-President Jorge Pacheco Areco became the new Uruguayan President. He implemented anti-inflationary measures which led to demonstrations and political agitation.

17. In the 1971 elections, the Colorado Party's candidate, Juan María Bordaberry, won the elections and assumed the presidency in a difficult context that ended in his overthrow in 1973. This was the year the army seized power and a dictatorship began that lasted until 1985. In 1985, Dr Julio María Sanguinetti, from the Colorado Party, won the first democratic elections after the dictatorship.

18. In the elections of 1989, the White Party won the elections, and Dr Luis Alberto Lacalle became the new President. In its administration, Dr Lacalle tried to modernize the State by presenting various bills, many of which were important milestones and are in force until today in the form of the Harbours' Act.

19. Between 1995 and 2004, the Colorado Party won two elections. The second period (from 2000 to 2004) was difficult for Uruguay, since it was affected by an overwhelming financial crisis. Even though the country was able to overcome the crisis, it reflected in the decreasing popularity of the Colorado Party in the 2004 election, which received its worst percentages in its entire history.

II. Cultural Composition

20. Uruguay is home to 3.3 million people, and approximately 88% of its population is of European descent. Uruguayans have descended from immigrants who came, mainly, from Spain, Italy, and Portugal, and as a consequence, Uruguay's major influences have been from these countries. Approximately 6% of the population is of African descent. The descendants of the original native population are a small minority.

21. The illiteracy rate is approximately 2% in Uruguay, the lowest in Latin America. However, only 30% of its population pursues university studies.

22. The country is secular, and freedom of worship is guaranteed by the Constitution. Catholics form approximately 66% of the population, though a major part of them are not practising. Approximately 2% of the population is Protestant and 1% is Jewish. Approximately 31% do not profess any religion.

III. Political System

23. Uruguay is a constitutional democracy in which the President is the head not only of the State but also of the government. Uruguay has a written Constitution, originally issued in 1830, which adopted the system of 'checks and balances' and 'separation of powers' articulated by Charles-Louis de Secondat, Baron de la Brède y de Montesquieu. The original text was modified several times and, consequently, Uruguay has had six Constitutions during its history (1830, 1918, 1934, 1942, 1952, and 1967). The last Uruguayan Constitution was deeply amended in 1996, but in no point in Uruguayan history did the Constitution reject the essential principles referred to above.

24. The President appoints the other members of the Executive Power, ministers, who are designated to various sectors of the country such as foreign affairs, economy, agriculture, and the army, among others.

25. The Uruguayan President is elected along with the Vice-President in one single ballot, for a period of five years. The Vice-President replaces the President in the event of the President's death, absence, or disability as well as when the President is temporarily absent due to travel. The President cannot be re-elected in the immediately following election, but he can run for presidency again after at least one administration has been headed by a different person. The President is elected by the people.

26. Uruguay, after the amendments made in 1996, became a two-round-system country. To win the presidential election, a candidate must obtain more than 50% of the authorized popular votes (cast by citizens). If this percentage is not reached by any candidate, the candidates with the highest and the second highest number of votes compete in a second ballot (*ballotage*) to win the presidential election.

27. The Congress resides in the General Assembly which is formed by two chambers: the Chamber of Senators and the Chamber of Representatives (*Diputados*). There are thirty senators and ninety-nine representatives. The Vice-President is also part of the Chamber of Senators as its President and is also the President of the General Assembly. Both Senators and Representatives are appointed for five-year periods in their positions and can be re-elected in a new, immediately following election.

28. The election of Congressmen is conducted through the system of closed ballots along with the presidential and vice-presidential elections. At least two representatives are elected for each department, with the election made specifically for each department. Senators are national candidates, and all candidates are the same for all departments.

29. The Judiciary is headed by the Supreme Court of Justice, whose members are appointed by at least two-thirds of the General Assembly, and each member is appointed for a ten-year period. Judicial Power is also formed by Appeal Courts and Trial Courts (*JuzgadosLetrados and Juzgados de Paz*).

30. Uruguay has been, since its independence, a centralized country in which the most relevant decisions are taken in Montevideo, its capital city. In the last few decades, Uruguay has begun a decentralization process seeking more balanced decision-making processes.

31. Local governments (the governments of the departments) have two major administrative bodies: the Executive Power headed by the Governor (*Intendente*) and the Local Assembly (*Junta Departamental*) that is the local Legislative Power. Offices are located in the capital city of each department.

32. The Governor is elected directly by the people in general elections that are separate from the national election. The Local Assembly is a one-chamber legislature formed by thirty-one members (*Ediles*) from which sixteen members belong to the winning party and the rest of the members are elected from the lists of the other parties according to the proportions of votes obtained.

33. Also, in certain towns of the countryside, local Committees are elected by the people or by the Local Assembly (with the support of the Governor), depending upon the relevance of the town.

34. Finally, as a new step seeking decentralization, the third level of local authorities was recently created in Uruguay in 2009. In certain towns which have more than 5,000 inhabitants, there are executive committees known as *Alcaldías* which have five members each, one of them being the President, who is referred to as 'Major'. Moreover, the capital city of Uruguay, Montevideo, was also divided into regions and *Alcaldías* were created for each one.

The most relevant feature of the Uruguayan Constitution related to Antitrust Law is the last sentence of section 50 which sets forth the following:

> Each trust either a business association or an industrial organization will be under the State's control. Furthermore, the State will foster decentralization in order to improve regional development and general welfare.

35. Even though a systemic law regarding antitrust is something relatively new for the Uruguayan system, this provision was laid down in the Constitution in 1952, and every statutory provision issued since then should have taken it into account.

36. For more than fifty years, the government kept procrastinating a systemic regulation of these issues, but it had been on the political agenda for the last ten years and a structured, modern legislation about antitrust was finally issued in 2007, as will be discussed later in this book.

37. The Uruguayan political system in the twentieth century was dominated by the two traditional parties (the Colorado-(Red)-Party and the White Party). The Colorado – Red – Party governed the country most of the time (during the constitutional periods) except for two periods when the government was formed by the White Party, which were from 1958 to 1966 and from 1990 to 1995.

38. During the decades of the 1940s and the 1950s, Uruguay was called the 'Switzerland of America', due to its unmatched economic prosperity at that time in the continent and due to other features that persist even today, such as banking secrecy, stability, neutrality in wars, among others.

Another reason Uruguay retains this *nickname* is because it recently ranked second in a list of less-corrupted countries in Latin America.

39. In 1992, Uruguay signed the most important regional Treaty in terms of integration, the South American Economic Organization (Mercosur) (*Mercado Común del Sur)*. The MERCOSUR was formed by Argentina, Brazil, Paraguay, and Uruguay, and according to the 2007 Report of the European Commission,[1] '(…) has promoted peace and stability, generated a high level political dialogue and strengthened internal and international cooperation'.

40. This Treaty, made on the basis of the experience of the European Union, was intended to be the doorway for a real integration among the countries of South America. The final goal was a common market in which countries could trade freely with each other and make common decisions about their products.

The MERCOSUR, so far, has not achieved this degree of development, but the idea of a common market is still in force. In fact, the 2007 Report of the European Commission[2] stated about this point:

> Although MERCOSUR still needs to make substantial efforts to reach its original goals, considerable progress has been made with its institutional framework. Today, MERCOSUR faces three major challenges: (i) improving its decision-making process and its capacity to implement and enforce common legislation, (ii) achieving the common market, and (iii) increasing the awareness and involvement of its civil societies in the regional integration project.

1. European Union Report. European Commission. Re: Mercosur. Regional Strategy Paper 2007–2013. 2 Aug. 2007 (e/2007/1640), 4.
2. European Union Report, *supra* n. 1, at 4.

41. The Colorado – Red – Party won its last election in 1999 and formed the first Uruguayan government in the twenty-first century. It tried to foster integration with other countries outside the region, such as Mexico and the United States (US), and promoted a liberal economic policy.

42. During this period, major financial problems hit Uruguay, causing one of the most serious social crises ever to occur in Uruguayan history. This situation affected the economy of the country as a whole and the Uruguayan middle class, and one of the twentieth-century features of the country was directly compromised.

43. This situation favoured a major change in the political history of Uruguay. For the first time ever, a left-wing political coalition, *FrenteAmplio*, won the elections and established more social initiatives, though there were no major changes in economic policies.

44. The *FrenteAmplio* party modified the foreign strategy and tried to relaunch the MERCOSUR Treaty by fostering regional cooperation. Even though this new strategy was applied, all new policies were applied with strict regard for Uruguayan Law.

IV. Population Statistics

45. The Uruguayan population is approximately 3.3 million but according to recent studies conducted in Uruguay, approximately 3 million Uruguayans live outside the country. The majority of the Uruguayan population, approximately 1.5 million people, live in the capital city, Montevideo, and its suburbs. The rest of the Uruguayan population lives in the other eighteen departments. Even though Uruguay is mainly agricultural, half of the country's population lives in the capital city and almost 95% of the whole population lives in the urban sectors.

46. The annual increase of the population for 2015 is estimated to be 0.6% and, consequently, the total population expected in 2015 is 3,676,092,000.

47. Other major departments in terms of population are Canelones, Maldonado, and Colonia.

48. Life expectancy is 76 years on average, being 73 for men and 80 for women. Ninety-eight per cent of the population has access to drinking water and 94% have access to hospital services.

§2. The Economic System

I. Historical Background

49. Uruguay is a small country that achieved, beginning in 1870, an important economic development when it found a capitalist mode of production, being a worldwide supplier of basic products, comprised mainly of livestock and certain agrarian products, features identified back in the colonial period.

50. The livestock production increased along with a strong protection of real property in the countryside and the development of transatlantic navigation mainly by the application of new technologies in meat preservation (which avoided spoilage caused by long trips to Europe). At this point, Europe increased its purchasing power as a result of the economic expansion, which was excellent for Uruguay's purposes.

51. Between 1875 and 1913, a production surplus occurred, and Uruguayan rural businessmen reinvested in the same agricultural sector. This situation was important to achieve a salary per capita similar to industrialized countries.

52. Nevertheless, economic development came to a halt due to the stagnation of livestock production by the early 1920s and the decline in the economy of the UK, which was one of the most important customers of the Uruguay's production. This period is considered by Alan Cage[3] to be the end of the state of prosperity which Uruguay had until 1913. The Depression began in 1913, due to the international financial crisis, which occurred alongside a reduction in Uruguayan exports, directly affected the Uruguayan economy. Prices fell and consequently, the wealth generated by the livestock sector reduced by almost 50% between 1913 and 1916. Export of basic products was blocked due to World War I, although prices increased during the conflict. Only in 1925 did Uruguay recover the levels of production it had reached before the crisis.

53. The said reduction made the connection between livestock production and the rest of the Uruguayan economy evident, since the crisis caused a 15% reduction in the industry. Furthermore, this occurred despite the economic protectionism applied by the Uruguayan government at that point.

54. After the big international crisis, triggered in the US in 1929, Uruguay began a modification in its economic structure by the early 1930s, with a protected industry which substituted import of products from foreign countries. This strategy created a stronger industry alongside a decadent livestock production.

55. The international crisis caused developed countries to stop producing industrialized products; hence, the Third World countries, Uruguay among them, had to

3. Alan Cage, *El Ciclo Económico*, Breve Historia Económica Del Uruguay, 3.

produce their own products, having to avoid imports as they were no longer available. This was deemed a positive development since local industry was fostered by the government, thus increasing the level of employment in the country.

56. Between 1945 and 1955, the Uruguayan economy grew in percentages that had never been achieved in its history, and wealth distribution was done successfully, hence making Uruguay one of the most thriving economies in Latin America.

57. This situation made the Uruguayan government initiate a process of acquisition of certain international companies that run, as a monopoly, companies that were truly important for certain strategic areas of the economy. Uruguay, as a strategy, anticipated that by establishing governmental monopolies, the benefits of the companies can be more easily accessed by the population. The milestone in this process was the acquisition of the railroad, which was once owned by England, by setting up a governmental agency to run the railroad in 1948.

58. The said process, accompanied by constitutional authorizations, is relevant in the history of Antitrust Laws in Uruguay, since with governmental monopolies in the most important areas of the economy, the idea of competition was not used as in the majority of the South American countries. This situation was about to change around 1990, not only in Uruguay but also in several countries of the region.

59. During the 1960s and the 1970s, a process of excessive investment in local industry, which was clearly uncompetitive in comparison with re-emerged developed countries and new strong economies due to a lack of updated technologies, sent the economy downhill. These problems and the fight for the distribution of the remaining wealth inherited from the 'happy fifties' produced an environment that created a conflict between organized employees and the government. This conflict was one of the reasons, generally seen[4] as the trigger for the *coup d'état* that occurred in 1973 and the twelve-year dictatorship which Uruguay suffered from, between 1973 and 1985.

60. In addition to the decline in the economy, there was a blatant reduction in the investment process in the industry. Capitals that in the past were invested within the boundaries of Uruguay were now transferred to foreign lands and more attractive opportunities in new economic sectors.

61. For these reasons, production was halted, unemployment rose, and inflation reached percentages that had never been seen in Uruguayan history. Uruguay went through several years of economic crisis, which had its milestone in the well-remembered *Quiebre de la Tablita* in 1982, a situation which occurred when the Uruguayan government established an artificial equivalence (without considering what had happened in the capital market) between the Uruguayan Peso and the American Dollar. In 1982, this equivalence was broken by the inevitable weight of the international market.

4. Alan Cage, *supra* n. 3, at 5.

62. After this painful crisis, a slow restoration process was begun by the end of the 1980s, not only for the country's economy but also for the country's confidence. In 1989, a strategy of 'structural adjustment' was launched and a market deregulation was imposed, as well as more flexibility in the relations between employees and employers.

63. Even though Uruguay did not issue antitrust rules at the beginning of the 1990s, this exact point in history is recognized by certain commentators[5] as the moment in which competition law was disseminated. In this period, it was incorporated by many jurisdictions, such as Brazil and Argentina, as a natural complement to liberalization and economic flexibility policies.

64. At this time, during the 1990s the economic model once applied by the Uruguayan governments, based on the import of products, was substituted by an export model – similar to the economic model used in Chile, New Zealand, and Ireland – one comprised mainly of commodities and services to the region.

65. This governmental policy strengthened Uruguay and its economic reputation from an international perspective as a supplier of raw materials and food. Moreover, Uruguay consolidated its position in South America as an expert in tourism, intellectual property, and financial services.

66. The said strategy evidently affected the industry, which had been a major part of the Uruguayan economy in the past, since its activity had been remarkably reduced. The most important industries went bankrupt during the 1990s, since without the protectionism applied decades ago, they were unable to openly compete with countries that had lower structural costs.

67. Based on this economic model, and due to the significant increase in banking deposits in the Uruguayan banking system, the economy grew between 1990 and 1998. After that, the country was affected by a recession which ultimately triggered the last major economic crisis Uruguay suffered, in 2002.

68. Since several countries in Latin America had suffered an economic/financial crisis before 2002 (e.g., the crises in Mexico and Brazil), the Uruguayan crisis of 2002 could have been predicted and hence avoided, but it was not. This was due to the fact that these crises had not affected the Uruguayan economy enough to foretell the Uruguayan crisis.

69. At that time, the parity continued between the Argentinean Peso and the US Dollar (one-to-one). Nevertheless, when the problems in Argentina began, with restrictions in money operations in Argentinean banks and transaction limitations in consumers' access to their deposits, Uruguay should have foreseen serious consequences in its banking sector (due to its dependence on the Argentinean market).

5. Ortiz Blanco, Luís; Maillo González-Orús, Jerónimo; Ibáñez Colomo, Pablo Y Lamadrid De Pablo, Alfonso. Manual De Derecho De La Competencia, Tecnos, Madrid (2008) 19.

70. Uruguay began in 2002 without any suspicion that such a major crisis was looming, in apparent tranquillity and with an economy with acceptable Economic Indicators.

71. It was only when the Argentinean citizens crossed the *Río de la Plata* to withdraw, in many cases, all the money from their deposits, that Uruguay finally felt the effects of the crisis.

72. To highlight some facts related to the Uruguayan crisis of 2002, it is important to point out the following:

(a) *Local Currency*: in January 2002, Uruguayan citizens exchanged Uruguayan Peso (UYU) 14 per US Dollar (USD) 1, while in September 2002, they exchanged UYU 31 per USD 1. This implies that the value of the US Dollar had doubled.
(b) *Unemployment*: during the same period, the Uruguayan unemployment rate increased from 14% to 19%.

73. Uruguay was going through a difficult time. Several Uruguayan banks and companies that Uruguayans had believed to be extremely strong went bankrupt.

74. To give another example, Uruguay had more than forty banks in its market in the year 2000 and currently, in 2012, there are only twenty-five approximately. The perception of Uruguay as 'the Switzerland of America' was razed to the ground, along with that of its banks.

75. Other explanations have been provided to interpret the serious crisis, outlined by Cage[6] as follows:

(a) The dynamic of the economic system. The productive period of the 1990s was simply over.
(b) The Brazilian and Argentinean crises with their economic devaluations.
(c) Reappearance of the 'foot-and-mouth' cattle disease.
(d) The economic policies which were seen as errors because they affected the profitability of Uruguayan companies.

76. Uruguay recovered from the said crisis and its economy stabilized. It seems that the country learnt some lessons from the economic mistakes made in the past, since Uruguay is among the few other countries which have not been affected by the global crisis that began in the US in 2008. In 2012, Uruguay was one of the two economies that grew during the crisis in South America and received several investment projects in 2008 and 2009, whose impact on the Uruguayan economy has been critical.

---

6. Alan Cage, *supra* n. 3, at 7.

77. Nowadays, investors need a perfect combination of factors to feel secure investing in a country, and essentially the following: political and economic stability, transparency and legal security, and an absence of corruption. At present, Uruguay is seen by international investors as an ideal place to invest in, owing to the existence of these factors and because the country respects the rule of law.

78. Uruguay was ranked by *Transparency International*[7] as the least corrupt country (along with Chile) in Latin America.

79. In fact, Professor Julio C. Porteiro[8] has stated that in a market, not only is the national offer important but also the international one. Hence, knowledge of the regional market in which an investment is made is an important prerequisite for the success of a project.

80. Investments are, currently, the most important source of development that Latin American countries have. Not only do small economies like Uruguay need investments to survive but also autarchic economies such as the Brazilian economy require investments to be, among other things, more efficient.

81. However, being open to foreign investments and avoiding protectionism are strategies that have to be combined with clear antitrust rules such as the ones the country issued in the last decade, to balance the goal of obtaining foreign investments with another important one of having a health market without any abuse of dominant positions.

§3. The Legal System

82. The country is politically organized as a republic, with a democratic government system that has three independent branches of power.

83. The Uruguayan legal system is based on statutory law passed by the Congress and ratified by the President. The most important source of law is the Constitution. There are specialized Courts with jurisdiction over civil, commercial, labour, criminal, administrative, and Family Law cases.

84. Uruguay is a civil law country where the stare decisis system is not applicable. Although Court rulings may guide other judges under the same circumstances, such rulings are not binding precedents as in the Great Tradition of the Common Law.

---

7. http://media.transparency.org/imaps/cpi2009/.
8. Julio Cesar Porteiro, *Evaluación de Proyectos de Inversión. Perspectiva Empresarial*, FCU, Montevideo (2003).

85. Uruguay strongly respects fundamental rights and has democratic principles and a republican government system. The country is organized on the basis of a written Constitution, which can only be amended pursuant to its legal provisions.

86. All amendments must necessarily end up in a plebiscite, and only with the voters' approval can the Constitution be validly amended.

87. The Constitution in force in Uruguay, nowadays, has the following essential components:

(1) Recognition of the fundamental rights of the person.
(2) Consecration of a republican government system.
(3) Limitations placed upon the public power.

88. The Uruguayan Constitution recognized the 'Separation of Powers'. Montesquieu[9] expressed in *The Spirit of Laws* that there are three powers that have to be organized in a coordinated way in which one power controls the other. This principle is closely linked to the idea of a democratic state and of the 'State of Law'.

89. Montesquieu stated that when the Legislative and Executive Power are vested in the same person, freedom of either is impossible.

90. An application of this principle is the so-called system of weights and counter-balances, which is the basis of the Uruguayan Constitution.

91. A practical example of this principle, which is part of the Uruguayan system, is that its Congress, in addition to its law-making duties, exercises major controlling powers such as, for instance, the power to demand reports from public authorities; to grant or refuse its consent to many decisions, including the appointment and removal of authorities; to act as arbitrator regarding controversies between public corporations and the Executive; among other powers.

92. Finally, another feature of the principle of 'Separation of Powers' is the independence of the Judiciary, also recognized by the Constitution.

93. Furthermore, judges have to be 'career judges' and make decisions without any pressure from the other powers.

94. Uruguay issued a Commercial Code and a Civil Code, in 1866 and in 1868 respectively, which were amended and modified by acts issued later in history. According to the Uruguayan system, Codes are issued as acts and consequently they can be amended or overturned by a later act.

---

9. Charles De Secondat, Baron De La Brède Et De Montesquieu, *DE L'ESPIRITU DES LOIS*, Ch. VI, Book XI, Ediciones Altaya S.A., Barcelona (1996).

95. Acts regarding Antitrust Law are clear examples of a complement to the referred Codes as they do not provide rules regarding antitrust.

96. Finally, the access to public tenders or purchases in the context of governmental bids is guaranteed in Uruguay. Obtaining public contractors for the government is, in general, pursued through open bids.

§4. Historical Background of Antitrust Law

I. Background

97. Antitrust Law is a work in progress in Uruguay, since it was not until the early 2000s that the Uruguayan Congress, along with the Executive, started to generate the framework which the legal system required on this matter. In contrast to other legal systems, such as the American legal system, which has decades of Antitrust Law enforcement behind it and a great case law tradition, Uruguay is still taking its first steps towards the development of Antitrust Law.

98. Until 1999, Uruguayan Law had merely a general antitrust rule embodied in its Constitution (section 50), according to which the government was to control commercial and industrial antitrust behaviours. This rule was extremely general, and its application was difficult in the absence of statutory law.

99. Between 1999 and 2001, Uruguay introduced three acts[10] that directly dealt with the question of whether or not the occurrence of certain events should be avoided in a healthy market. Instead of a general Antitrust Law, several statutory rules were passed, which were revolutionary for the Uruguayan Law at that point.

100. Two relevant Acts were passed in 1999, which had an impact on the development of the new Uruguayan Antitrust system. On the one hand, the 'Act of Great Surfaces' was passed and on the other, certain regulations were included in the Uruguayan Patent Act.

101. The Act of Great Surfaces (No. 17.188) dated 8 September 1999 organized a previously local control proceeding in order to set up businesses that use an area of 300 square metres or more for the commercialization of foodstuffs and household products. According to the referred Act, before authorizing the projects of this kind of businesses, a Local Committee needs to rule about the consequences and influence of this new business in the area in which it would be established.

102. Furthermore, the Uruguayan Patent Act (No. 17.164) passed on 18 August 1999, in its section 60, sets forth that the National Agency of Intellectual Property

10. Act 17.188 passed on 8 Sep. 1999; ss 13, 14 and 15 of Act 17.243 passed on 29 Jun. 2000 and ss 157 and 158 of the Act. 17.296 passed on 21 Feb. 2001.

can grant 'Mandatory Licenses' when it can prove that the patent holder has committed an antitrust practice, or abused the rights granted by the patent, or committed any sort of abuse of a dominant position.

103. These two acts confirmed that the Uruguayan legal system was increasingly interested in antitrust issues and, in this context, Act 17.243, a multipurpose act, was passed, which set out specific antitrust rules in one of its chapters. This Act, which expressed the first serious intent in Uruguayan history to regulate this matter, was deemed insufficient.

104. Section 13 of the said Act set forth the principle of free competition by restating the general constitutional principle. Section 14 directly addressed the issue of prohibited antitrust practices. To achieve this, it restricted agreements among agents of the market to assure free competition and prohibited the abuse of a dominant position and laid down rules regarding some specific cases of prohibited practices.

105. Furthermore, section 15 of the Act authorized the Executive Power to organize the general system by initiating a proceeding to solve disputes that could arise from the practical implementation of the Act.

106. Finally, Act 17.296, dated 16 February 2001, was passed to complement the previous Act. It set forth the sanctions to be enforced by the government in relation to the businesses that infringed any provisions of Act 17.243.

107. This system was effective until July 2007, when the Congress passed a new Uruguayan Antitrust Law which overturned the former law by regulating a whole new structure through a complete act that incorporated in its sections a comprehensive regulation of antitrust issues.

108. During the almost seven years in which Acts 17.243 and 17.296 were in force in the Uruguayan system, the development of the antitrust system was clearly insufficient. It is fair to say that the country was yet to get accustomed to these new rules, in the absence of precedents in Uruguay. For this reason, the development and enforcement of the new system were not as extensive as had been expected.

109. The most crucial fact was that, in this first period, antitrust issues were finally raised and different scholars began to study the rules and proposed new ways of increasing the effectiveness of antitrust rules. Some of the problems worth mentioning were the inexperience of the entire system along with the fact that the governmental agency created, did not have any previous exposure to real antitrust cases, which greatly slowed down the development of jurisprudence that was actually applicable to the act.

110. Notwithstanding the foregoing, one of the major obstacles to the enforcement of these provisions was the lack of an antitrust culture that dealt with and understood antitrust issues.

111. In fact, during this period, there were not any significant cases. However, it is significant that one of the few cases in which antitrust provisions were enforced deals with this lack of antitrust culture referred to above.

112. The said case involved an organization of broadcasters, which decided to publish in a newspaper an article referring to what it considered a 'lack of ethics' in one of its members. In the context of the article that aimed to disclose the alleged unethical behaviour of one of its members, the organization inadvertently revealed that the association's members agreed to fix certain prices when offering their services to the government in public bids, which is one of the prohibited conducts under the Uruguayan Antitrust Law.

113. As a consequence, the alleged lack of ethics in one of the members, which had been publicly disclosed and considered unethical, was the correct conduct as per the Uruguayan Antitrust Law. The rest of the members, who had considered this conduct unethical and had decided to publish it in a newspaper, were fined for the violation of the Antitrust Law by the enforcing Authority acting ex officio.

II. Act 18.159: New Uruguayan Antitrust Act

114. Finally, on 30 July 2007, the Uruguayan Congress passed Act No. 18.159 (hereinafter 'Act') which embodies, in itself, the general rules regarding Antitrust Law.

115. As mentioned above, until the approval of this Act, there were acts which contained certain specific regulations regarding Antitrust Law. These acts set forth the principle that all companies were subject to competition rules and stated the forbidden conducts, enumerating, without limitation, specific hypotheses. Also they laid down the powers of the Authority in charge of controlling forbidden acts and conducts, as well as the applicable sanctions.

116. These provisions have been revoked by the said Act (passed on 30 July 2007) and are therefore no longer in force.

Notwithstanding the foregoing, the essence of the old system survived, although improved by the Act which is wider in scope and addresses more issues.

117. In a brief overview of the Uruguayan region, it can be said that both Brazil and Argentina followed the US system. Argentina struck down Act No. 22.262 and passed Act No. 25.156 in 1999, which not only sought to avoid the abuse of a dominant position but also sought to control economic concentration when it could affect competition, by requiring pre-merger authorizations. Brazil has also followed the US system earlier (Acts 4137/62, 8884/1984, and 9781/1990) asking for pre-merger authorizations.[11]

---

11. Jaime Berdaguer, *Control de la Concentración Empresarial*, Estudios Sobre Defensa De La Competencia Y Relaciones De Consumo, Fcu, Montevideo (2008).

Part I. The Structure of Antitrust Law and Its Enforcement

Chapter 1. Sources of Antitrust Law

§1. National Sources

I. General Principles

118. As the Act sets forth in section 1, its purpose is to promote the welfare of consumers and users 'by means of the promotion and defence of competition, the stimulation of economic efficiency, freedom and equal access conditions for companies and products to markets'.

119. The reference to '*consumers and users*', as the Act's final beneficiaries, can seem to be a simple declaration or a minor detail. However, it is relevant and it can have important consequences, since it may form the basis for the argument that, in certain cases, practices can appear anticompetitive when they are not. This is certainly possible when a conduct, which can objectively be included in the category of the conducts considered anticompetitive by law, ultimately benefit such class, that is, 'consumers and users'. In this case, this specific practice should not be considered to be against the antitrust rules.

120. For instance, if in Uruguay there is an oligopoly of sugar, and the four firms that distribute sugar enter into an agreement wherein they intend to reduce the final price of sugar since they need to fiercely compete with sweeteners in the market, this practice appears anti-competitive. In the final analysis of this case, only four sugar distributors agreeing to fix a specific price may directly affect the competition between sugar and sweeteners, hence this can be considered as a prohibited practice.

121. However, according to the interpretation pointed out, this decision will finally benefit the customers, who will be able to access this essential product by paying less. Consequently, this practice can be considered legal under the Uruguayan Law owing to the benefits the consumers receive from it.

122. It should be specifically taken into account by agents of the market, that the Act's final purpose is to develop competition itself, and not specific conflict between or among economic agents.

123. The principle that underlies these provisions is that the development of competition ultimately improves the efficiency of economic agents, which consequently will benefit consumers, who are, as mentioned, the final target of this Act.

124. In the hypothetical circumstances previously discussed, it is evident that a decision among agents that can be considered as prohibited in itself, can be deemed to be perfectly legal, provided it ultimately positively affects the final customers.

125. Furthermore, the Act lays down in section 2, a general principle that had been included in the former Uruguayan Antitrust regulation, according to which all markets are subject to the principles and rules of free competition, with the exception of the limitations set by law due to reasons of general interest.

126. When the Act refers to limitations that can be set by law due to '*reasons of general interest*', it is taking into account the case of public monopolies in certain areas, such as public transportation, supply of drinkable water, among others. The said areas are considered 'public services', and they are either forbidden to individuals or permitted only in specific cases when the government grants authorizations that allow individuals to perform them.

127. As a corollary of this general principle, the Act forbids certain practices which could affect competition.

128. The second paragraph of section 2 deems the following to be forbidden practices: 'the abuse of a dominant position, as well as all practices, conducts or recommendations, either individual or coordinated, which have an effect or purpose to restrict, limit, hinder, distort or obstruct the current or future competition in the relevant market'.

129. In this context, one of the biggest innovations of the Act, as had not been regulated in the previous legislations mentioned, was the creation of a government control mechanism in Merger & Acquisition (M&A) transactions, which intends to prevent economic concentrations that can lead to anticompetitive behaviours. This kind of control had been in existence in the US since the Sherman Act of 1890 and in different countries of Latin America as well as, recently, countries in Europe. However, given both the lack of antitrust regulation in most of Uruguayan history and the prevailing international patterns, some kind of government control in M&A transactions was deemed necessary and was ultimately created in 2007.

130. A new act regulating antitrust matters is being discussed by the Uruguayan Parliament. The project sets forth the need to obtain the government's authorization before M&A transactions, when certain conditions are met. The content of this new draft bill will be explained in the chapter referring to M&A operations.

131. In conclusion, two of the Act's main concerns are as follows: (i) to ensure that competition takes place effectively; and (ii) to ensure that it occurs in an adequate manner, since only then does economic efficiency improve and consumers are able to access better conditions.

132. Finally, Antitrust Law is usually confused with other legal areas such as the good or bad faith evidenced by certain economic agents in their attempt to obtain positions in the market.

133. These attitudes, even if they are relevant from a legal perspective and could be deemed Unfair competition, and also form grounds for legal actions, they are not, in principle, within the scope of the Act.

134. These attitudes would only be relevant from the perspective of Antitrust Law if their effects were such that they could cause a restriction or distortion of the market. If they do not have such effects, it does not matter how unlawful such conducts could be, they will still be irrelevant from the perspective of Antitrust Law.

135. Unfair competition does not have any specific regulation for Uruguay and has been typically treated under the general principles of Tort Law. In our country, to be considered an unfair conduct, the following three requirements have to be met:

The existence of a situation in which competitors are involved.
Conduct which goes against commercial loyalty.
Conduct which, if performed, can harm other competitors.

136. While the rules regarding unfair competition regulate the relations among competitors, defending those competitors whose clientele has been stolen due to conduct against commercial loyalty, Antitrust Law is interested in the market, defending not certain firms in particular but the whole system.

II. Public Policy

137. According to section 1 of the Act, the Act is expressly deemed to be a public policy statute, which means that no agreements between private parties can disregard the provisions of the Act.

§2. International Sources

138. As has been discussed, Uruguay is one of the founder members of the South American Treaty named MERCOSUR (Spanish acronym of Mercado Común del Sur, Portuguese Mercosul, acronym of Mercado Comum do Sul, or Common Market of the South), which was created in line with the experience of the European Union.

139. Even though it was expected to achieve the kind of development seen in Europe, the development in South America was slower, mainly due to the size differences between its members (Brazil, Argentina, Paraguay, and Uruguay). At present, the usefulness of the MERCOSUR is under analysis, especially in the big countries. This question has been raised, since it is considered that the said Treaty's structure makes it impossible for its member countries to enter into direct treaties with other countries.

140. However, the MERCOSUR is still fully effective as an imperfect '*Customs Union*', which implies a stage prior to the regional common market.

141. The said issues, connected with the political presence of the said Treaty, also influence the effectiveness of the law of MERCOSUR.

142. According to Article 42 of the '*OuroPreto* Protocol', any piece of legislation from any of the bodies of the Treaty is mandatory for all the members.

143. MERCOSUR has three intergovernmental organs that have decision-making powers, as follows:

(1) The Council of the Common Market.
(2) The Common Market Group.
(3) The MERCOSUR Trade Commission.

144. The first organ mentioned above is the most important one, which issues *Decisions*, whereas the second one issues *Resolutions* and the third one issues *Directives.*

145. After the *OuroPreto* Protocol and the decision of making the law of the MERCOSUR mandatory to the states that are members of it, a specific problem arose, since all of the member countries have different legal systems. Even though the method of incorporating the different laws into any legal system is applicable to all of them, the way in which this is executed varies from one country to the other. In all countries, a national statutory decision is necessary.

146. For this reason, scholars have discussed whether or not MERCOSUR law is an independent body of laws or if it is to be deemed as international law that is yet to be ratified.

147. The decisions of the MERCOSUR organs shall be taken by consensus and in the presence of all the member countries (Article 37 of the *OuroPreto* Protocol).

I. Regulations

148. In 1994, Decision 021/94 by the Common Market Council about antitrust issues was issued. The objective of this regulation was to set common guidelines for the 'competency defence' in the MERCOSUR. This regulation fostered a coordinated action aiming to prevent various practices against free competition within the territory of the Member States of the MERCOSUR Treaty.

149. Before passing this regulation, a subcommittee created to analyse antitrust issues in the MERCOSUR's member countries had prepared a memorandum which enlisted different criteria that could be used as the basis for common legislation.

150. Decision 021/94 was two-pronged: first, it laid down different rules in order to protect competition in MERCOSUR, and second, it also regulated a general proceeding to fight against antitrust practices in the countries of MERCOSUR.

151. Chapter III of the above decision structured in three sections the issues that have later been repeatedly ruled in the different national legislations regarding competency law. These three sections are as follows: (a) prohibition of arrangements among the economic players of the market which try to prevent, restrict, or distort competency and free access to the market; (b) prohibition of a dominant position; and (c) control of M&A transactions that can affect more than 20% of the relevant market and can produce antitrust effects.

152. As previously mentioned, this MERCOSUR regulation has also dealt with the regulation of a proceeding intended for the members of the Treaty. According to the above decision, each member country, in whose jurisdiction an alleged violation of competency law is found, has to initiate an investigation within a maximum time period of thirty days. This investigation has to be conducted on the basis of the national legislation on this matter and the corresponding sanctions that can be imposed in accordance with the national law.

II. Guidelines

153. After passing the *OuroPreto* Protocol in 1994, the members of the MERCOSUR signed the so-called *Fortaleza* Protocol in December 1996, which laid down an extensive group of guidelines aimed towards a general and common policy in the South American region in terms of Antitrust Law.

154. The said protocol laid down as mandatory that each country creates a specific Antitrust Agency; strong enough to fight against violations of the national law. Also, it provided that member countries were to share common principles in regard to competition policy.

155. Due to the reasons previously discussed, the said protocol did not create a singular agency that would cover all the member countries, with supranational effects, since this was not possible in the prevailing stage of the Treaty. The effectiveness of the said guidelines of the regional Treaty can only be ensured by each country's national agency's power to enforce the guidelines.

156. As previously discussed, although Argentina passed its first Antitrust legislation back in 1919, and Brazil in 1962, competition issues became truly relevant in these countries only in the 1990s, when important privatization processes were developed.

157. In Brazil, Act No. 8884, passed in 1984, restructured the Brazilian Antitrust Laws and gave more relevance to the '*ConselhoAdministrativo de DefesaEconomica*' as the head of the antitrust system. This agency had an extremely important role in the regulatory reforms made in Brazil in the areas of energy, oil, and telecommunications by the end of the 1990s.

158. As for Argentinean law, it was amended in 1946 and in 1980, but the relevant reform was made in September 1999 by the passing of Act No. 25156, which created the Antitrust Tribunal empowered to regulate the market. With an enlarged scope of application, this Act introduced significant new provisions, such as merger control and the autonomy of the Antitrust Authority.

159. Uruguay and Paraguay had a slower process of application of the Fortaleza Protocol, but by the first few years of the 2000s they also introduced their own rules in connection with antitrust regional policies.

160. Furthermore, it is relevant to mention that one important goal of the above protocol is to prevent antidumping measures among MERCOSUR countries. According to José Tavares de Araujo Jr.[12] since the signing of the Treaty of Asuncion in 1991, Argentina has brought thirty-eight antidumping actions against Brazil, two against Paraguay, and one against Uruguay; while Brazil has brought two investigations against Argentina and two against Uruguay.

§3. Secondary Sources

I. Regulations

A. Decrees

161. According to the Uruguayan legal system, all and any statutes, which may need a further development of their provisions to be made by the administration, can be regulated by Decree 404/2007 issued by the Executive Power. The said faculty is laid down in section 168 of the Uruguayan Constitution.

162. In this respect, Decree 404/2007 regulates, in detail, all the different aspects included in Act No. 18.189.

12. José Tavares De Araújo JR Conference on 'Competition Policy in Infrastructure Services: Second Generation Issues in the Reform of Public Services' organized by the Infrastructure and Financial Markets Division and the Multilateral Investment Fund of the Inter-American Development Bank, Washington, DC, 23–24 Apr. 2001.

163. According to the hierarchy principle, this decree cannot overrule what has been stated in a statute and must at all times be *secundemlegumcommunen.* In the event of any contradiction, the statute shall prevail and the decree must be disregarded.

164. Although these kind of decrees are issued by the Executive Power, the head of the government, they should not be deemed at any time to be an order by the organs subject to its hierarchy; on the contrary, they can and should be disregarded by any organ subject to its hierarchy in the event that a contradiction arises between the statute and general principles.

II. Guidelines

A. General Provisions of the Commission

165. One of the most important advances in the Uruguayan Antitrust system is that the new regulations (section 16 of Decree 404/07) have given to the organ in charge of applying antitrust rules ('commission' or 'agency') the faculty to enact general and abstract rules regarding antitrust.

166. These general rules cannot contradict any provision of a decree or statute, or general principles and should only have the purpose of further facilitating the application of antitrust rules.

167. In the event that they contradict any of the said rules, they should be disregarded. If necessary, these general rules can be challenged, as will be explained further in this monograph.[13]

168. Although the commission has not used this faculty yet, it is of great importance because it gives to the commission the role of a regulatory agency in addition to the power to enforce.

B. Particular Instructions of the Commission

169. Finally, the commission is entitled to order the individuals to act in a specific manner, and these orders are binding on any particular individual. This faculty has not been used yet and is not common in our system in which previously only the Central Bank was entitled to address the orders to the entities regulated by it.

170. The 'particular instructions' may contain abstract rules to be viewed only by the entities and/or individuals to which they are addressed.

---

13. *See* the Ch. titled: *Challenging of the Administrative Decision.*

171. Although our antitrust system is, in general, based on the idea of not interfering with the market unless sanctions are required to be imposed for any infringement, the fact that the commission can issue particular instructions and promote competition allows a new and more active participation of the commission in the entire design of competition.

172. However, the traditional approaches may turn to be more reactive than proactive in this area of practice.

173. In the event that these particular instructions effectively contradict any other provision, they should be disregarded in all cases, respecting the general principles of interpretation. If necessary, these particular instructions can be challenged as can all and any administrative decisions.

§4. Source: Relation and Hierarchy

174. Uruguay applies the hierarchy of norms developed by Hans Kelsen, placing the Constitution at the top of the legal pyramid, followed in order of prevalence by acts, decrees, and governmental decisions.

175. As has already been explained, although Uruguay is an active member of the MERCOSUR, which as international organization passes various norms intended for all its members, these norms do not have a force superior to national norms. Furthermore, they do not have direct application within the Uruguayan territory unless incorporated through a national norm.

176. As a corollary of what was explained, if a MERCOSUR decision is, for instance, incorporated into the Uruguayan legal system as a decree and the latter collides with an act passed in Uruguay or a constitutional provision, the Constitution and the act will prevail over the decree even when the MERCOSUR decision is a piece of International legislation.

177. Whether the MERCOSUR decision was incorporated through a national act or not, in such a case, it will be valid and effective in Uruguay and will prevail if in conflict with decrees or other norms which are inferior in hierarchy as compared to governmental decisions.

178. In the above-mentioned instance, the act will not be applied if it is declared unconstitutional by the Uruguayan Supreme Court. In Uruguay, unconstitutionality is declared for any case which has been decided on the basis of a norm that is against the Constitution; such a case is required to be filed with the Supreme Court, which will decide on a case-to-case basis.

179. However, it is clear that if unconstitutionality is declared, any individual who has been harmed by the application of this provision, that was declared unconstitutional, will ask the Supreme Court for the same decision. Typically, when an act is declared unconstitutional by the Supreme Court, the government fosters modification or the direct overturn of the norm in question, to prevent new unconstitutional actions.

§5. Role and Authority of Precedents

180. Uruguay, as has been previously explained, is a civil law country and, consequently, a stare decisis system is not applicable.

181. The legal system is based on written statutes; case law does not have a mandatory prevalence on future actions. Courts are fully independent of the political power.

182. The common law and the civil law systems are the results of two fundamentally different perspectives of the legal process.

183. In the civil law tradition, the main principles and rules are included in codes and statutes, which are applied by the Courts. Consequently, codes and statutes prevail over case law, which is only a secondary source of law. In the civil law system, the law is not created by judges as it is in the case of the common law system.

184. The case law in civil law systems does not have any binding force. As has already been said, the doctrine of stare decisis does not apply to civil law Courts and, consequently, Court rulings are not binding on lower Courts in subsequent cases, nor are they binding on the same Courts, and it is not unusual that Courts review their conclusions in subsequent similar cases.

185. In civil law, the main function of the Courts is to interpret the law as contained in a specific statute, without being bound by the interpretation of the same norm made by other Courts, whether higher or lower. The corollary of the system is that under civil law, the Courts do not create the law, but only apply and interpret it.

186. In practice, however, the higher Courts' decisions, mainly the Supreme Court rulings, influence lower Courts, since trial Court judges usually anticipate the risk of their decisions being reversed by higher Courts if they contradict the latter's decisions.

Chapter 2. Scope of Application

§1. Territorial Reach

187. The Act has a wide scope of application. The general principle of free competition applies to all individuals and legal entities, public or private, national or foreign, which perform economic activities, lucrative or not, in the Uruguayan territory.

188. In principle, as any other Uruguayan Act, it has territorial enforceability and is mandatory for Uruguayan judges as well as for arbitrators or foreign judges who have to apply Uruguayan Law.

189. However, the Act included an extraterritorial provision by stating that it is applicable, in the same terms, not only to situations which occurred in the Uruguayan territory but also to situations in which the economic activities were carried out abroad, if such activities have full or partial effects in the Uruguayan territory.

190. In fact, section 3, paragraph 2, reads as follows:

> This Act will be applicable to any person that pursues economic activities abroad as long as the effects of this activity were fully or partially felt in the Uruguayan territory.

191. This provision laid down the extraterritorial effect of the Act by extending the application of the above-mentioned provisions to areas outside the Uruguayan boundaries. Although the said provision makes sense since there are cases in which decisions made abroad impact the Uruguayan market, it is evident that the enforceability of these provisions is not easy.

192. Uruguay does not have bilateral or multilateral treaties regarding Antitrust Law enforcement, which could ease the application of this extraterritorial provision. Provided a Uruguayan judge is required to enforce the Uruguayan Law within MERCOSUR's boundaries, in such a case, the bodies of the regional Treaty may intervene, facilitating the enforceability of a local law upon a firm in a country which is not a member of the Treaty. However, while dealing with a conduct by a company outside MERCOSUR, in order to enforce Uruguayan Law in a non-member country, the Uruguayan judge must initiate the general proceeding, which is typically time-consuming and the application's effectiveness will depend on country's legal system.

§2. SPECIAL SECTORS

193. The Act set forth in its section 2, as was established in the previous regulation on the subject, the general principle that '*all markets are subject to the principles and rules of free competition*' with the exception of the '*limitations established by law due to reasons of general interest*'.

194. By '*limitations established by law due to reasons of general interest*', it must be understood, as previously said, those activities to which individuals cannot have access in principle, such as, legally established monopolies and activities which the law qualifies as 'public services' (e.g., public transportation, drinkable water supply, basic telephony). Such activities are either forbidden to individuals or require an act of concession from the state to enable individuals to perform them.

195. Consequently, in principle, antitrust rules cannot be applied in these sectors and competition cannot take place freely herein.

196. However, it would be erroneous to consider that state-owned companies performing services in these special sectors are not bound by antitrust rules. On the contrary, though these companies have been awarded economic privileges in special areas of economic activity they usually perform activities in related areas where competition is free.

197. The lines demarcating reserved areas from competition areas are not always clear and the temptation to abuse may cause these state-owned companies to participate in abuse quite often. If this happens, the state-owned companies can be sanctioned by the commission, since Antitrust Law applies to all individuals and all legal entities, public or private, national or foreign, which perform economic activities, lucrative or not, in the Uruguayan territory.

198. In terms of special sectors, section 27 of the Act is highly significant. In accordance with this section of the Uruguayan Antitrust Act, competition cases involving banks or other companies with special government regulations should be examined by the special agency. In fact, the Uruguayan Central Bank, the Energy & Water Services Agency, and the Communications' Agency will be the agencies in charge in connection with antitrust cases that involve their areas and not the Uruguayan Antitrust Agency.

199. In accordance with section 27 paragraph 3, these agencies should not follow rules different from the ones laid down in Act No. 18.159; though they have certain specific norms. However, due to the peculiarities of the entities involved, additional information may be sought by the agencies. For instance, in banking mergers or acquisitions, typically, the Uruguayan Central Bank asks for further information regarding the deal in order to estimate not only the future composition of the market after the deal (which generally entails that one or more banks shut down) but also the strength of the group that is taking a slide of the market, considering a crisis scenario.

200. Finally, it is interesting that in accordance with section 27 of the Uruguayan Antitrust Act, cases involving other companies with special government regulations, other than banks, are required to be examined by special agencies and not by the Uruguayan Antitrust Agency.

§3. State-Owned Enterprises and Public Utilities

201. Uruguay has a history of supporting state monopolies in several areas in which direct foreign equity participation is prohibited by law. Privatization has been widely opposed by the governments and in the 1990s, when the executive raised the question of privatization regarding some of the state monopolies, the initiative was turned down by the people exercising their vote against it.

202. Even though Uruguay has defended its public companies, several state-owned entities have entered into associations with foreign-owned companies to provide specific services for a specified period of time.

203. Notwithstanding the foregoing, as regards local regulation, private power generation is currently allowed, and the state-owned power company, UTE, still holds certain monopoly rights in the business.

204. Other examples are the state-owned oil company, ANCAP, which is the only importer and refiner of petroleum products in the country, and the state-owned telephone company (ANTEL). Cellular service is provided by ANTEL under the commercial name of ANCEL. A local wireless loop system, the installation and maintenance of public phones, data transmission, and some value-added services have been granted to the private sector.

205. All Uruguayan ports are operated by and administered through the national port administration, Harbour's Authority (ANP). Many port services were, however, privatized in 1992. A state enterprise, Drinkable water State's Company (OSE), controls most water and sewage services in Uruguay except in some resort areas on the coast. In 1996, 51% of the state-owned airline PLUNA was sold to the private sector.

206. In 1996, the state monopoly in the insurance sector was eliminated. Foreign investors are treated as nationals in privatization/concession programmes and are allowed to participate in any stage of a privatization/concession.

207. As has already been pointed out, in accordance with section 3 of the Act, Antitrust Law is applicable to state-owned companies. However, since monopolies continue to exist in Uruguay, Antitrust Law does not apply to state-owned monopolies. Furthermore, as will be discussed below, monopolies (in fact) are not prohibited in all cases in Uruguay. Avoiding a monopoly, even when there is no market for other players will certainly be something artificial that can eventually make it impossible for customers to access certain products. In these cases, Uruguayan Antitrust Law permits the existence of monopolies in fact.

§4. Sensible Effect and De Minimis

208. Although not established as a requirement in the current regulations, the effects of a conduct should, at the very least, be 'relevant' for the antitrust provisions to be enforced. A distortion of the market which can only be admitted theoretically but cannot be visualized or evidenced otherwise should not entitle the commission to apply any sanction.

209. In the past, Act No. 17.243 expressed that antitrust rules should only be applied when the situation in question '*causes relevant damages to the general interest*'.

210. This rule was not clear since it could be interpreted in various ways and was, in fact, interpreted variously. On one hand it was said that there could not be any infringement to the Antitrust Law provisions unless damages were effectively caused and deemed relevant. On the other hand, it was pointed out that it made no sense to wait until the damage was caused. A third interpretation explained that the intention was to sanction only conducts that could potentially cause serious damage or that generally cause them.

211. However, the provisions in force do not contain a similar requirement.

Chapter 3. Overview of Substantive Provisions

212. The substantive provisions of the Uruguayan Antitrust Law are gathered in three important sections of Act No. 18.159.

213. The Act sets forth in section 2, as was previously regulated by the former act on this matter, the general principle that 'all markets are subject to the principles and rules of free competition' with the exception of the 'limitations set out by law due to reasons of general interest' to the extent already explained.

214. As a consequence of the general principle previously mentioned, the Act forbids certain practices which could affect competition.

215. In fact, the second paragraph of section 2 considers the following to be forbidden practices: 'the abuse of a dominant position, as well as all practices, conducts or recommendations, either individual or coordinated, which have an effect or purpose to restrict, limit, hinder, distort or obstruct the current or future competition in the relevant market'.

216. With minor changes in the wording, the said solution is similar to the one used by the former Uruguayan Antitrust Act.

217. Two important differences in comparison with the former system are as follows:

218. The Act expressly includes the prohibition of conduct which has the '*purpose*' of restricting, limiting, etc. This means that all conduct performed purporting a restriction of competition are forbidden. The Act primarily takes into account the intention with which the conduct is performed, hence a certain conduct would be forbidden even when it has not been able to achieve the antitrust result inasmuch as it has been performed with the intention of causing such result.

a. The requirement that the distortion of the market causes a relevant damage to the general interest, as a criterion for conduct to be considered forbidden, has now been eliminated. Considering this elimination, any forbidden act or conduct which affects the relevant market will be punishable even though any special damage has not been caused.

219. Section 4 lays down that the practices expressly described by this section in nine paragraphs will be considered to be 'prohibited practices'. However, this is a non-restrictive list which means that there may be other behaviours that can be considered to be 'prohibited practices' under Uruguayan Law.

220. Although the different prohibited practices regulated by the Act will be discussed throughout this book, it is relevant to briefly summarize the provisions, as follows.

221. Section 4 lays down the nine different behaviours that are expressly considered prohibited practices under Uruguayan Antitrust Law:

(1) To agree or impose, directly or indirectly, prices to buy or sell products, as well as other provisions, in an abusive way.
(2) To limit, restrict or agree, in an unjustifiable way, the production, distribution and technological development of assets, services or productive sources in detriment of competitors and consumers.
(3) To unjustifiably apply to third parties different conditions in case of same transactions, putting one party on an unequal situation towards its competitors.
(4) To subordinate entering into an agreement to certain additional promises that, considering their nature or commercial practices cannot be considered as typical in this type of agreements.
(5) To coordinate submission or abstentions in submitting proposals to public bids, public or private price contests or the like.
(6) To avoid that competitors gain access to essential infrastructure to produce, distribute or sell goods, services or production tools.
(7) To unjustifiably hinder that new competitors gain access to the market.
(8) To unjustifiably establish exclusive zones or activities to which certain economic agents cannot gain access.
(9) To unjustifiably refuse selling goods or rendering services.

222. Finally, the same section points out that the same practices shall be considered illegal if they had been agreed upon by unions or associations of economic agents.

§1. Restrictive Agreements

223. As has been previously discussed, section 4 of the Act, sets forth which practices are, in general, considered to be against the Uruguayan Antitrust Law. It is crystal clear that restrictive agreements that make it impossible for an individual or company to access a certain part of the market are illegal since they unjustifiably exclude new competitors that, ultimately, can reduce prices or increase the quality of certain types of products. The goal of Uruguayan Law is to ensure that the market is not in the hands of some entities which may intend to divide it and refrain new competitors from offering their products.

224. In Uruguay, section 4 paragraph B of the Act prohibited certain practices among which vertical restrictions are included. It states that it is considered as illegal to limit, restrain, or illegally agree upon the production, distribution, and technological development of goods, services, or productive factors, against the interests of competitors and consumers.

225. The new Act excluded from the final paragraph of the section, the generalized statements as had been made in the overturned antitrust section of Act No.

17.242. The former system set forth, as an additional requirement for antitrust practices to be considered illegal, that they cause a '*relevant prejudice to the general interest*'. The controversy around this general expression began during the discussion of the bill in the Uruguayan Congress.

226. Many commentators had said that this expression had made the regulation's enforcement almost impossible. Other scholars tried to make a less demanding interpretation that enabled the practical implementation of the Act.

227. Nevertheless, this problem was solved by the wording of the new section, which excluded, in general, this kind of generality in wording.

228. The Uruguayan literature has been discussing whether or not the imposition, direct or indirect, of purchase or sale prices or other transaction conditions on the consumer can be considered as a restrictive clause. In fact, by setting prices or stipulating terms that can be considered as abusive, an agent of the market may exclude other agents in a vertical structure, ultimately affecting consumers.

229. Most commentators consider that the threshold is the benefit of the final consumers. If the price or other kind of clauses that imply certain level of restrictions is imposed in an abusive way, they can be considered illegal.

230. In fact, upon closer examination, exclusive clauses clearly restrict the market, since certain distributors can sell only one brand or a specific product due to the agreement signed with a principal. However, it is clear in Uruguay that this kind of restriction is, in principle, not prohibited and yet is totally extended in the Uruguayan market, as will be further discussed.

231. As has already been explained, the ultimate beneficiary of the law is supposed to be the consumer. Considering the situation, an exclusive agreement is not, in itself, a way to affect consumers. Provided that the market has more than one distributor who can ensure that the product in question is accessible to consumers, exclusivity will not create a restriction.

232. In fact, the test is whether the system can ensure that its consumers get the best products at the best prices. In the case of a distribution agreement whereby the principal prevents the distributor from selling other competitive products by applying an exclusivity clause in the contract, and there is only one distributor in a city (as is most likely in the countryside), the customers will be affected. In such a case, the exclusivity clause will be considered restrictive.

233. However, if we consider a market with various distributors that can be considered as various and independent players, if one of them enters into a contract with a principal setting forth an exclusivity clause, it will not be considered to be against Antitrust Law. The other firms competing with the firm that acquired an exclusive distributor will still have the opportunity to sell their products through the other available distributors.

234. The key to determine whether or not an agreement with an exclusivity clause can affect competition is the opportunity customers will have to buy other brands if they decide to do so.

235. It will be deemed as a restrictive practice also if a specific firm tries to acquire the exclusivity of all the distributors of a relevant market, since the effect will then be the same, as the customers will then have the opportunity to buy only one type of products.

In this regard, a recent case (*Resolution 32/2012 of 2 May 2012*) decided by the Uruguayan Antitrust Agency, set forth that an agreement entered into a kinder garden and a tailor's shop, whereby the referred shop would be the exclusive store authorized to sell uniforms of the kinder garden was illegal. The reasoning was that the fact that only one tailor's shop makes in exclusivity the uniforms, which are mandatory for students, by restricting other shops from tailoring and selling them, is against Uruguayan rules on Competition.

236. In conclusion, Uruguayan Law admits the risks of accepting exclusive dealing due to its potential to harm customers. However, it is not a practice prohibited in itself, but is prohibited only when, due to the exclusivity clause, the customers cannot buy other types of products of the same quality as the ones sold by the exclusive distributor.

237. Another situation that has been taken into account by the Uruguayan administrative jurisprudence and mainly by the Uruguayan doctrine is the so-called *price fixing*. It appears that a restrictive arrangement in such a context can affect consumers, whether it is accomplished through vertical or horizontal price fixing.

238. In the former legislation regarding competition law in Uruguay, vertical price fixing was normally only considered illegal when there were no reasonable justifications for that arrangement, which hindered the enforcement of the law. To be considered as restricted, the former legislation required that the price imposition or other conditions had to be carried out '*in an abusive way for the consumers*'. However, even when horizontal agreements were not expressly mentioned, they were considered to be covered by the former legislation, from a practical perspective.

239. Even though we will come back to this concept below, currently the most important example considered in Uruguay to be restrictive agreements performed by concerted actions is that of group boycotts, which imply a concerted action to eliminate competitors in an illegal manner.

§2. DOMINANT UNDERTAKINGS

240. There are some unilateral types of conduct targeted to prevent competitors from entering a relevant market, by restricting access to essential facilities or attacking minor competitors using predatory practices.

241. Section 6 of the Act lays down that one or more companies or individuals are considered to be in a 'dominant position' when it/they can substantially affect the market, regardless of the behaviour of the rest of the competitors, buyers, or commercial providers.

242. Hence, what is banned by the Act is the *abuse* of the dominant position, which means the use of this position to gain illegal advantages or to harm other agents, which would not have happened without this particular power over the market.

243. As a consequence, dominance itself is not prohibited, only its abuse – as is the case in the European Union.

244. Dominant undertakings are considered 'unlawful behaviour' if an agent of the market, by abusing its position, hinders other competitors in their efforts to start or continue to compete.

245. A dominant undertaking is definitely mentioned in the general rules of unlawful economic concentrations set forth by the Uruguayan Law and is, in fact, prohibited. This means that an economic concentration that leads to a dominant position is prohibited.

§3. CONCENTRATIONS

246. The term 'economic concentration' is generally defined as an operation that modifies the structure of the market by introducing a relevant change in the weight of the market power. Moreover, an economic concentration, typically, affects the ownership or the control process of the companies competing in a specific market sector.

247. A change of control is necessary for a concentration to take place in the antitrust sense of the word.

248. Several questions need to be raised in order to determine if an economic concentration can modify the market structure, for example: the number of companies, the independence of their administrators, among other factors. For these reasons, economic concentrations have been the subject of regulation in most jurisdictions which have competition laws.

249. Section 7 of the Act provides that the Uruguayan Antitrust Agency is required to be notified of every act of economic concentration within certain thresholds set by law. In the same section, it is said that potential acts of economic concentration are:

those operations which imply a modification in the control structure through: mergers of companies, acquisition of shares, membership interests or participations, acquisition of business as an ongoing concern, total or partial acquisition of corporate assets, and any other type of legally valid agreement which imply transferring the control of all or part of the economic units or enterprises.

250. An economic concentration (whether it matches the thresholds will be below) must be notified to the Antitrust Authority. According to the Act, there is an obligation to notify the corresponding Uruguayan Agency of acts of economic concentration, ten days before such acts are executed by companies, provided that such acts fulfil any of the following requirements. It is relevant to point out that it is not required that both the conditions are fulfilled simultaneously. If even one of them occurs, the notification process is triggered. The two conditions are as follows:

(1) When as a consequence of the transaction, the market share of the combined entity equals or exceeds 50% of the relevant market.
(2) When the gross annual invoicing, in Uruguayan territory, of the participants in the transaction equals or exceeds USD 75,000,000 in any of the preceding three financial years.

251. Notwithstanding the above, section 8 provides four exceptions in which there is no obligation to notify, even when some of the above-mentioned conditions are met. They are the following:

(a) The acquisition of companies wherein the buyer already had at least 50% of its shares.
(b) The acquisition of bonds, debentures, obligations, any other security issued by the company, or shares with no voting rights.
(c) The acquisition of only one company by only one foreign company which previously did not possess assets or shares of other companies in the country.
(d) Acquisitions of companies, which have or have not declared bankruptcy, which have not registered any activity within the country in the previous year.

252. The purpose of the notification is not to receive an authorization of the transaction (which is required in certain cases when a 'de facto monopoly' or 'monopoly in fact' occurred), but to notify the antitrust commission of the existence of an economic concentration that meets the thresholds. The result being that the Antitrust Agency cannot prevent the deal.

253. Regarding concentrations, the Uruguayan Congress largely discussed which of the two models regarding M&A authorizations/notifications, applied in the world (*ex ante* and *ex post*), was more suited to the Uruguayan characteristics. There were supporters of both sides, and none could refute the other's stand. In light of this dichotomy, the solution was that the control should be made neither *ex ante* nor *ex post*. A hybrid solution emerged from the discussion of the bill, since it is neither a typical pre-merger authorization nor an ex post facto resolution. The Uruguayan Act called for a 'Notification' that was required to be made in certain specific situations.

254. The main purpose of this notification is to notify the commission of the economic concentration, so that the commission can be informed about market sectors in which anticompetitive practices or abuse of a dominant position may most likely occur.

255. As a consequence of this proceeding, the commission will not have the power to challenge a merger, while this is definitely not a test of illegality. The purpose here is to declare that due to this transaction, antitrust situations are likely. It is a mere notice to the government. No event that can be considered to be against Antitrust Law has as yet happened to date, but due to the peculiarities of the deal, the legal system necessitates a particular redress of the situation post the deal.

256. Currently, a bill modifying the existing regime over economic concentrations is being studied by the Uruguayan Parliament.

257. The bill under study sets forth that the approval of the concentration by the Antitrust Authority will be necessary, not only when as a consequence of the concentration a monopoly in fact is created, like the regulation in force currently established, but also when the economic concentration may create market structures that limit the competition in detriment of consumers.

258. In such cases, the Antitrust Authority will have sixty days to approve the operation, subordinate it to the fulfilment of certain conditions or deny it. If after the sixty days term the aforementioned Authority did not pronounced, the concentration will be approved.

§4. Other Prohibitions

259. As has been previously explained, section 4 of the Act lays down the nine different behaviours that are expressly considered to be 'prohibited practices' under Uruguayan Antitrust Law, but the list is not comprehensive. There may well be other prohibitions separate from the ones expressly stated by the Act.

260. For instance, although the abuse of economic dominance is not expressly prohibited under the Uruguayan Law as an illegal practice, it can be deemed as an example of antitrust behaviour if it ultimately affects consumers.

§5. TEST OF ILLEGALITY

I. Per Se Prohibitions and Naked Restraints

261. In general, in Antitrust Law there are two systems to deal with the question of whether or not a specific behaviour is prohibited. The first one is the 'per se' system, in which several behaviours are condemned and the second one is the '*rule of reason*' wherein the law simply lays down general rules without identifying any specific kinds of conduct.

262. The 'per se' system is more suited in applying the law because it is simple and the companies can foresee the consequences of its application to them. The drawback is that many new practices can easily escape identification under the 'per se' system and its definitions.

263. The Uruguayan Act chose a system that is neither a '*rule of reason*' system nor a 'per se' system. It is a combination of the two systems, as will be discussed below.

II. Balancing Tests

264. Under the law of certain countries, balancing tests are prescribed in order to measure the consequences of any prohibited conduct. For example, in the banking sector there is a common application of a balancing test between competition goals and goals of banking regulation, when Antitrust Law is applicable to banks.

265. In Uruguay, there is no specific provision regarding balancing tests, and the conduct should be gauged by the Uruguayan Agency by taking into account the general principles laid down in the Uruguayan Act. In fact, the factors to be taken into account by a judge, when deciding whether certain behaviour can be considered illegal, are the abuse of a dominant position and whether the practice can ultimately harm the consumers.

266. The Uruguayan legal system selected a system that is neither a 'rule of reason' system nor a 'per se' system. It is a combination of the two systems, which in fact, exhibits the predominance of the per se system, given that the Act takes into account various situations. However, there is a certain amount of influence of the 'rule of reason' system, since some criteria, which have been laid down in section 2, consider the following to be 'prohibited practices': the abuse of dominant position, as well as all practices, kinds of conduct or recommendations, individually or concerted, that aim to restrict, limit, hinder, distort, or prevent the current or future competition in the relevant market, or have any such effect(s).

267. As a consequence, Uruguay does not have 'per se prohibitions' or 'naked restraints'. In fact, a specific conduct will be deemed illegal not just in itself, but inasmuch as it affects some of the principles previously pointed out.

III. Merger Tests

268. There is no separate substantive test applicable to a merger to determine whether it is anticompetitive and, therefore, whether it can be completed. The same hybrid test, as already discussed, laid down by Uruguayan Law is also applicable in case of mergers.

269. If two or more companies together affect the market by creating a restriction in the customers' accessibility to a specific product or products, it is not the merger itself (which cannot be challenged) but the subsequent behaviour of the surviving company or the entity that emerged from the merger, that can be considered to be anticompetitive.

270. In fact, as regards mergers, the issue in Uruguayan Law is whether or not certain thresholds have been reached, because here the law anticipates that a possible anticompetitive situation could be triggered and, consequently, the agency will pay special attention to the behaviour of the new entity or the entity surviving after the merger.

271. As already explained, to find out whether or not a merger between two or more companies in a relevant market can affect the competition environment, the Uruguayan Law set two thresholds as follows:

(1) When as a consequence of the transaction, the market share of the combined entity equals or exceeds 50% of the relevant market.
(2) When the gross annual invoicing in Uruguayan territory of the participants in the transaction equals or exceeds USD 75,000,000 in any of the preceding three financial years.

272. In the event that one of the thresholds is achieved in a specific deal, interested parties have to give notice to the Antitrust Agency with the effects that will be explained in detail.

Chapter 4. Overview of Main Notions

§1. Undertaking

273. According to the European Union Law, an 'undertaking' is any entity engaged in an economic activity to which anticompetitive law is applicable, regardless of its legal structure or the manner in which it is financed.

274. Uruguayan Law does not have a similar/corresponding term, and according to the Act, what is required to be analysed is not the legal structure or the type of entity, but its behaviour in a certain relevant market.

275. However, the Act in fact laid down that its regulation is applicable to all markets 'with the limitations set by law due to reasons of general interest' (section 2).

276. By 'limitations set by law due to reasons of general interest', the Act refers to those activities to which individuals cannot, in principle, have access, such as legally established monopolies as well as activities which the law qualifies as 'public services'. Examples of 'public services' are: public transportation, drinkable water supply, etc. These activities are either forbidden to individuals or require an act of concession by the government to allow individuals to perform them.

277. Therefore, a public entity, in principle, can be considered to be an undertaking, inasmuch as there is no specific act in Uruguayan Law excluding it due to reasons of general interest.

278. In conclusion, in spite of the fact that the Act, in principle, is applicable to all 'undertakings', the government, in certain cases, is not a player from an anticompetitive perspective, since, for instance, it can continue to have monopolies due to reasons of general interest.

279. The reason why, in certain cases, non-profit organizations cannot be subject to anticompetitive law, is the 'social function' they have in society. The justification is essentially similar to the one used by Uruguayan Law to exclude the Uruguayan state from the scope of the Uruguayan legal system in certain instances.

280. Nevertheless, section 3 of the Act refers to 'all individuals and legal entities public or private, domestic or foreign, which develop activities with or without profit interests', which obviously includes non-profit organizations.

281. There are no specific rules in Uruguayan Law granting privileges to non-profit organizations due to their social function. If a non-profit organization such as a high school (typically organized as a civil association) gathers an important part of the market by performing prohibited practices, the Act will be applicable.

282. Pursuant to the Act, an individual can be considered to be an 'undertaking', since the Act's definition of 'undertaking' includes any individual as a potential undertaking.

283. If a group of companies act together in a deal or behave in an anticompetitive manner as a group, such group would be considered to be only one undertaking for the purposes of Antitrust Law, although such group would comprise of various legal entities.

284. Furthermore, the question that arises is whether or not the liability can be extended to individuals or entities which have not participated directly in the prohibited practices.

285. In principle, the general rule in Uruguayan Law is that the liability is imposed on the individual and/or legal entity, except in certain unusual cases.

286. However, section 19 of the Act lays down a special liability of the directors of entities that participated in prohibited practices, by granting the agency the power to impose economic sanctions on directors as well, along with the companies.

I. Extension of Liability

287. Section 19 of Act No. 18.159 lays down an important variation to the previous regime. This section leaves open the possibility of extending the liability for anticompetitive practices performed by legal entities to the members of the board of directors and legal representatives as well as to the controlling legal entities and the members of their board of directors and legal representatives.

288. In the case of the members of the board of directors of a legal entity and legal representatives of it, their liability is subject to the condition that they actively contributed in the development of the anticompetitive practice. However, this condition is not applicable to the extension of the liability to the controlling legal entity.

289. It must be noted that when extending the liability to the controlling legal entity, the Act refers to 'legal entities', but when extending it to the board of directors and legal representatives, the Act refers to 'controlling company', instead of using the term 'legal entity'.

290. This creates a distinction since both terms cannot be deemed to have the same meaning. For example, governmental entities (*EntesAutónomos* and *Sevicios-Descentralizados*) of the state's commercial or industrial domain, and also some non-governmental public entities are not 'controlling companies' but 'controlling legal entities'.

291. This is not a minor issue since many of these entities own 100% of many commercial companies which compete in the market.

292. As a result, it must be concluded that the liability for prohibited practices of the controlled legal entity will be extended to the board of directors and the legal representatives of its controlling entity only in those cases wherein the controlling entity is a private commercial company (i.e., 'company'), but will not be extended if the controlling entity is a governmental entity (i.e., 'legal entity' but not a 'company').

293. It is important to point out that when referring to 'extension of liability' it implies a situation wherein individuals are jointly and severally liable along with the primary offender.

§2. Relevant Market

294. The Act correctly introduces into the Uruguayan legal system the concept of 'relevant market'. This concept in Antitrust Law refers to the 'scope' of the competitive activity which should be considered, for example, when determining if an agent has a relevant position, if its conduct could be considered to be anticompetitive, etc.

295. According to Gavil,[14] the principal direct technique for identifying substantial market power is to measure the elasticity of demand for the products of the firm believed to possess a monopoly. A relatively less elastic demand would indicate considerable power to raise prices above competitive levels and hold them there without experiencing a significant loss of customers.

296. The Merger Guidelines of the Department of Justice and the Federal Trade Commission of the United States (1992) (hereinafter 'Merger Guidelines') has defined 'relevant market', in what was considered by the Uruguayan scholar Camilo Martinez Blanco[15] as the best legal definition of 'relevant market' ever.

297. The goal of the definition is to facilitate a prediction as to whether a merger or an acquisition can possibly result in the exercise of a dominant position. Under the Merger Guidelines approach, the 'relevant market' is formed by the minor group of products wherein a hypothetical monopolist of all of them can profitably increase the price slightly. The idea is that in a competitive situation, no company can find it profitable to slightly increase the prices without fear of migration of all its customers to competitors.

298. In the Uruguayan Act, section 5 lays down that for the purpose of evaluating whether a practice is or is not competitive, the relevant market in which such

14. Andrew I. Gavil, William E. Kovacic & Jonathan B. Baker, *Antitrust Law In Perspective: Cases, Concepts And Problems In Competition Policy*, 462 (Thomson-West 2002).
15. Camilo Martínez Blanco, Grandes Cadenas, Poder Dominante Y Defensa De La Competencia. Fcu (2001) 38.

activity is performed should be determined first. This means that a practice cannot be considered to be anticompetitive in itself but only with respect to a certain market.

299. Thus, it cannot be said that the 'beverages market' has been affected, without any further specification, since that would be inadequate from a technical perspective. It should be noted that soda beverages do not compete with alcoholic beverages; and even then, not all alcoholic beverages compete with each other, and so on. In each instance, the products of each class should be specified.

300. The Act indicates certain factors to be analysed when determining the relevant market. This enumeration is not limited to the factors mentioned therein, since it clearly states that the said factors are as follows, 'among others': (i) the existence of substitute goods or services; and (ii) the geographical area comprised by the market.

301. The reference to the 'existence of substitute goods or services' is related to the concept of 'cross-elasticity of demand' which the high or low disposition consumers may have in consuming one product as a substitute of another one, for example, due to small price variations. When such elasticity is high, it can be concluded that both products are part of the same relevant market.

302. With respect to the 'geographical area comprised by the market', the Act clarifies that this refers to the 'scope of effective competition' of a good or service. In this sense, it is clear that a bakery in the city of Rivera (in the Uruguayan countryside) does not compete with one located in the capital city, Montevideo. However, it is not as clear if instead of a perishable good, the product in question is an electric appliance of high economic value. Also, these circumstances could vary with time.

303. Therefore, another criterion which should be considered in the determination of the relevant market, which was not expressly taken into account by the Act and which ought to have been considered, is the passage of time. Markets are constantly redefined by technological advances, the possibility of exchange and replacement of one product for another, differences in the preference of goods, etc. In this sense, continuing with the previous example, let us think about the market penetration experienced by packaged bread. Although it was unthinkable some time ago, bakeries in Montevideo and Rivera today experience competition even from hundreds of kilometres away. As such, the relevant market should necessarily have a defined time frame.

304. Finally, it should be noted that the agency, in a recent resolution dated 12 May 2009 (No. 2/009) ruled, construing section 5 of the Act, that in order to gauge if certain practices affect the relevant market where they take place, it is necessary, along with other factors, to consider the substitute products or services and the territory.

305. The Resolution, in dicta, laid down that when analysing substitute products or services, they must be considered not only from the seller's standpoint but also from the buyer's standpoint.

Moreover, in the *Resolution No. 67/013 of 21 May 2013*, the Uruguayan Competition Agency stressed the relevance of the geographic aspect, in order to define Relevance Market, by ruling that in a case involving bars and pubs of a resort town (Punta del Diablo in Rocha) the relevant market considered to analyse the case is compounded by the bars, restaurants (that open at night) pubs and the like located in Punta del Diablo.

§3. Market Power/Dominant Position

306. Regarding these concepts in section 6, the Act expressly defines 'dominant position' as follows: one or various agents have a dominant position in the market when they can substantially affect its relevant variables independently of the conduct of its competitors, buyers or suppliers.

307. Unlike in other countries, in Uruguay the dominant position is not linked to any special market share, and it does not presume or imply, per se, any infringement to Antitrust Laws.

308. In fact, it should be understood that the Uruguayan market is so small that many times the sectors involved reasonably do not have more than one or two players, simply because more players would imply a non-efficient display of resources from an economic point of view. In such cases, competition could lead to adverse effects rather than economic benefits.

309. Prof. Martinez Blanco[16] has maintained that a firm has a dominant position in a given market when vis-à-vis a particular product or service it is the only supplier or buyer within a territory, or even when it is not the only one, the rest are not serious competitors.

310. In order to clarify this idea and to fully understand the Uruguayan context, it is relevant to consider section 13 of the Mexican law of Competition, which lays down the requisite elements to determine the presence of a dominant position, which can be used from the Uruguayan perspective as well, even though the Uruguayan Act did not expressly provide a list such as this.

The referred elements are as follows:

(a) Analysing the participation of a given player in the market and if any player can unilaterally set the prices or restrict product supply in the relevant market. Also, the competitors' inability to commercially compete with it.
(b) Existence of restrictions to the entrance into the relevant market.
(c) A player's own access and its competitors' access to the products.

16. Camilo Martínez Blanco, *Grandes Cadenas … supra* n. 22, at 40.

(d) Recent behaviours.

I. Monopolies

311. In connection with the idea of 'dominance', the idea of 'monopoly' needs to be explored, as it is important for understanding competition law in Uruguay. It is relevant to note that Uruguay has granted legal monopolies to public entities, and this is quite contradictory to the general principles of competition law, even for countries with strong state structures.

312. Anticompetitive laws purport to create an environment of pure competition without any monopolistic competition in which monopolies and oligopolies can play by their own rules. In an atomized market with several players, all of which have different costs and objectives, the situation is certainly beneficial to consumers. In a monopoly, a product has only one price whose payment is the only way to access the product. As a consequence, there is no competition present to force the monopolistic seller to lower the prices.

313. An oligopoly is no different, because its members can set the prices without any interference. Hence, if the oligopoly chooses to set high prices, there are no small companies in the market to compete and cause the big companies to lower their prices.

314. In certain cases, as already discussed, provided there are no other options for monopolies to exist in Uruguay, the 'monopolies in fact' must ask the government for a special authorization to act in the market. Typically, this situation arises when in a particular territory, there is not enough space for more than one player, and to fight against the monopoly would lead to the elimination of a product or service from the market, which will adversely affect the customers' interests.

315. Furthermore, a possible situation wherein an oligopoly can be deemed to be legal is when it is very expensive to enter into a business sector such as the banking business, and the company would require millions of dollars to establish a branch. In these cases, it is possible that the market can have only a limited number of banks, and this situation will lead to a sort of legal oligopoly. It is obvious that the behaviour of this oligopoly will be controlled in order to determine whether or not any anticompetitive conduct has been performed.

316. In the said context, it is necessary to be especially aware of exploitative practices owing to the power a big company can have, which can ultimately lead to a monopoly or an oligopoly, eliminating competitors in a relevant market that can absorb several competitors. In these cases, the intent to eliminate competition is with a view to acquire an unlawful dominant position, and consequently, it would be deemed to be illegal as per Uruguayan Law.

317. When discussing monopolies, it is worth distinguishing between legal monopolies and monopolies in fact.

318. Legal monopolies are a restriction on the liberty of all inhabitants, and such kind of restriction can only be determined by statute and to the extent that the solution is in public interest. In particular, section 85 paragraph 17 of the Constitution provides for these requirements.

319. From a strict legal standpoint, monopolies can only be constituted in the Uruguayan system in economic areas and for the purpose of obtaining economic revenues.

320. However, in Uruguay there is another category called 'public service' which, from an economic standpoint, produces nearly the same result, since it ensures that individuals cannot freely carry out certain activities. For example, public transportation or water supplies are 'public services'. To the extent that these 'public services' are also restrictions to liberty, an activity cannot be deemed so unless a statute expressly states it.

321. Public services may be conducted by individuals only if they have been granted the right to do so by the government, usually after bid proceedings.

322. In some other cases, the applicable law provides that the government should render the service itself without being entitled to involve any third party. As a consequence, in this scenario, only a governmental entity is entitled to render a 'public service'. This is the case with drinkable water supply, after the constitutional amendment to section 47, passed in 2004. As per the Uruguayan domestic approach, the provision of these services should be considered to be 'public services in exclusive regime' rather than monopolies.

323. The difference between monopolies and 'public services in exclusive regime' cannot be perceived from an economic point of view. However, it should be pointed out that from a legal standpoint, it would not be correct to declare any services as 'public services' other than those services which deal with those necessities of the community which cannot be postponed.

324. In this sense, the authorization for casinos can constitute a monopoly but never a 'public service'. The distinction is important because the majorities needed in the congress to approve an act declaring an activity as a monopoly are higher than those needed to declare an activity as a 'public service'.

325. The concept of 'monopoly in fact' is entirely different. In some jurisdictions, a company is deemed to have a monopoly when it has a market share close to 100%, or for example, above 90%. In Uruguayan Law, there is no similar interpretation and hence, the correct interpretation of 'monopoly in fact' should be the traditional interpretation, according to which, there is no monopoly unless only one player holds 100% of the market share.

§4. Agreements and Concerted Practices

326. In general, the idea of 'concerted practices' used in American law and in the European Union is performed by undertakings which have not reached a formal agreement but, without it, have constituted by direct or indirect contact a coordination whose intention is to exercise certain influence in the market.

327. In the Uruguayan Antitrust Law, there is no need for any written agreement, and concerted practices can be reached without formal understanding. In our view, the simple consciousness of being part of a concerted practice may be enough to hold a player responsible.

328. In foreign jurisdictions, it is common to find distinctions between these categories: participation, concerted practice, simple consciousness of a practice in common, etc. However, the Uruguayan Antitrust Law does not have the necessary development behind it to address the said distinctions.

329. In any case, a conduct which cannot be deemed as an agreement may fall within the concept of 'concerted practice' or others like 'recommendation' or in a residual concept such as 'any practice'.

330. This means that a unilateral recommendation obviously cannot fall within the definition of 'agreement' since in this case there is no mutual consent, from a contractual standpoint, extended by both parties, but can fall within the general concept of a 'concerted practice', due to which the Uruguayan Act acknowledges this possibility by adding the general expression 'any practice'.

331. The important fact is that any of the said conducts would imply responsibility in the event that they cause or were intended to cause restrictions or distortions in actual or future relevant markets (section 3 of Decree 404/07).

332. Even though these practices can happen either in horizontal or vertical agreements, Uruguayan Law is considering the idea of agreements among competitors on the same level of production.

333. However, we think that, in certain cases, vertical agreements can be considered to be within in the definition, and the Act does not make any distinction between the situations.

334. Also, there is no indication in the law or in case law on the treatment of intra-group agreements. As previously stated, groups of companies are treated as one economic entity for antitrust purposes in Uruguay, and consequently intra-group agreements are not relevant from the perspective of Antitrust Law.

§5. RESTRICTION OF COMPETITION

335. According to Antitrust Law, competition should take place in a manner that could bring progress and benefit consumers. Although the provisions refer to several situations as different: to impede competition, limit, hamper, or distort it, the sense of all and any of these situations should be deemed to be included in the concept of restriction of competition.

336. It is not possible to provide examples for all and any kinds of restriction of competition that can happen, but it is useful to remember that competition should be as free as possible and should tend to improve the efficiency of the market players. Attempts of market players to take advantage of positions by other means are possibly restrictions of competition.

337. There is no legal concept such as 'relevant restriction' in Uruguayan Antitrust Law.

338. Also, it is relevant to point out that there is no provision in the Uruguayan Law similar to the European rule of *de minimis* in general terms. If an agreement that is signed has a restrictive object, but does not have any significant impact on competition due to its negligible effect on the market, it can, in principle, be considered to be in violation of Uruguayan Law.

339. The only thresholds that are stated by Uruguayan Law are in relation to merger cases, as already discussed.

340. As a result, when a judge reviews a case involving a prohibited practice that entails a violation of the law but does not affect a significant part of the relevant market, the judge has to apply the law relating to 'prohibited practices' if the relevant market is affected in any way.

I. Economic Efficiency

341. 'Economic efficiency' is a key concept in Uruguayan legislation. It refers to the need to determine how the conduct examined may impact the economy as a whole, in terms of the damage and/or the benefit it could cause, before deciding whether or not it should be deemed an infringement of antitrust provisions.

342. Although Uruguayan Law does not establish any type of thresholds to determine if a certain case should be examined in the light of anticompetitive law, it is interesting to analyse the cases from an economic perspective, though from a different standpoint.

343. Economic efficiency can be considered as a restriction on the application of the law, regardless of the relevant market. For instance, in a case when the entire relevant market is affected, if the consumers are not harmed, the case cannot be considered anti-competitive, even if a prohibited practice is performed.

344. However, the existence of economic efficiencies does not mean that consumers are not affected by an anticompetitive behaviour; the issue is that they can be positively affected by it. A practice may be anticompetitive and can produce economic efficiencies at the same time.

345. The point here is that since the ultimate target of the law is the protection of consumers, certain practices that may be technically unlawful would not be challenged by the agency, due to the benefits the customers receive from the said practices. This hypothetical behaviour cannot be part of a temporary scheme to eliminate competitors (for instance) because this, ultimately, will adversely affect consumers.

346. For instance, if in a specific territory there are two providers of the same product and they decide to set low prices due to the commitment they have towards the community, this action, at first glance, can be termed an unlawful practice. However, ultimately, this agreement on prices will favourably impact the consumers.

347. According to the Act, not only are those abusive practices prohibited when performed by an economic agent holding a dominant position in the market, but also every practice which has the effect or goal of restricting the competition, regardless of the participation of the latter or other agents in the market. Hence, abusive practices can arise not only from a dominant position but also from agreements.

348. As already explained, the Act will consider certain restrictive agreements to be unlawful whether or not the offender(s) achieved their goal. Furthermore, any kind of unintentional conduct that ultimately has a restrictive effect will also be considered to be a restrictive agreement. As a result, even though a specific conduct is not accompanied by the intention to achieve a restrictive result, if the latter was reached the conduct will be considered unlawful. In this case, the purpose of the agent is disregarded, being necessary only to consider the final effects over the market.

349. To determine if an act can be considered restrictive under Uruguayan Law, as previously explained, it will be necessary to consider whether the relevant market has been affected.

350. For instance, in the case of a restrictive act performed by a group of economic agents that have a dominant position, it will be certainly considered unlawful under Uruguayan Law.

351. Gerardo Caffera[17] has maintained that a restrictive agreement obtained by abusing a dominant position is peculiar due to one extrinsic characteristic, which is

---

17. Gerardo Caffera, *El Negocio Jurídico y la Legislación Nacional de defensa de la competencia (antitrust)*. Anuario de Derecho Civil Uruguayo, Tomo XXI, 588.

the power exercised by one of the parties over the market. However, it is essentially identical to any other contract. It is the contract's qualification as an instrument of the exercise of an economic power which makes the contract against antitrust regulations.

352. Another important issue to consider is that according to Uruguayan Law, the relevant beneficiary to be protected is the market, the competition itself and not a competitor in particular. For this reason, if any conduct of an agent affects a specific competitor without having any effect(s) that cause limitation or restriction in the market, the practice should be deemed to be legal.

353. As is obvious, the subject of discussion here is the consequences of certain effects on the market in the eyes of the anticompetitive law. However, an action as the one previously referred can be deemed illegal under the law of unfair competition.

II. Legal Analysis of the Restrictive Conduct

354. As already mentioned, Uruguayan Law ruled out the 'per se' system and chose a peculiar 'rule of reason' as its system. This implies that the Antitrust Agency is required to review the conduct in the light of the principles set by law.

355. For this reason, not every conduct that appears to be anticompetitive will have this characteristic. It will be necessary to analyse the reasoning behind the conduct and whether or not it has any sort of commercial justification. A specific conduct will not be justifiable if it is performed for the purpose of gaining illegal advantages or harming a competitor so as to affect competition.

356. Section 2, subsection 3 of the Act lays down that in order to find out if certain practices are anticompetitive, the agency should consider certain factors, as follows:

(a) If the conducts produce revenues of economic efficiency of the agents, economic units, and companies involved.
(b) The possibility of obtaining the same results in a different manner.
(c) The benefit that is received by the consumers.

357. The Uruguayan Agency has flexibility, under these rules, to find out whether or not certain conduct is anticompetitive. Considering the factors mentioned by law, there may be certain restrictive agreements that can, ultimately, be beneficial for consumers. In such a case, the agency can decide that a conduct that is apparently anticompetitive is found to be legal.

358. For instance, there may be a case in which two competitors in a relevant market significantly reduce their prices. At first, this conduct can be considered to be a restrictive agreement due to its potential to eliminate competitors and ultimately affect the competition by fixing an exorbitant price. However, if after certain period of time the prices remain low, the measure will ultimately benefit consumers, which is the goal of the antitrust system. As a consequence, this conduct will not be considered to be anticompetitive.

359. The above situation will not be considered to constitute a restriction of competition, since in accordance with section 2, subsection 3, the agency is required to consider the third factor (c) in ruling out an anticompetitive scenario.

§6. Monopolization and Abuse of Dominance

360. Regarding the concept of abuse of dominant position, the law provides that the said abuse is committed when the agent/s act/s 'in a wrongful manner with the purpose of obtaining advantages or causing damages to others, which they could not have obtained or caused if they did not have a dominant position'.

361. In the Uruguayan legal system, there is no reference to the said abuse in economic terms, which means that the abuse of the dominant position can be deemed to have happened regardless of the monetary amount involved.

362. As Prof. Marcelo Amorín[18] maintains, the idea of abuse is linked to the idea of 'being undue' or 'incorrectness'. In case of dominance, the Uruguayan Act requires an analysis that goes further than the mere prohibited practice. Not only the action but also its consequence must be considered, regardless of the amount of damage caused.

363. Also, it is relevant to point out that typically, the abuse of a dominant position is performed intentionally. However, there is no specific rule in Uruguayan Law that requires the intention of causing damage to be considered as abuse. The intent to abuse the dominant position is not relevant, and the concept of abuse is independent of subjective intent. The Uruguayan Act seems to require an intention to gain an illegal advantage.

364. The Act refers to the abusive behaviour performed by a dominant firm. A non-dominant firm cannot be held liable for the 'abuse' as ruled by section 2 of the Act, because it is reserved for dominant firms. However, all undertakings, whether dominant or non-dominant are subject to the Act and its principles and especially, to the rules regarding prohibited practices. In the case of non-dominant firms, a judge should examine the practice to decide whether or not it can be deemed anticompetitive, but not the abuse. The latter is relevant only in the analysis of dominant firms. Hence, in certain cases, a unilateral practice by a non-dominant firm can be considered to be unlawful under the Antitrust Law.

18. Amorin, Marcelo, *Abuso de Posición Dominante e Imposición de Precios, Estudios sobre Defensa de la Competencia y Relaciones de Consumo.* FCU, Montevideo (2008), 99.

365. It is crystal clear that the majority of unlawful practices set forth by section 6 of the Uruguayan Act are supposed to be performed by dominant firms. Nevertheless, there are certain actions, such as the imposition of certain conditions, not connected with the business, in the signing of an agreement that can be legally performed by non-dominant firms.

I. A Relevant Case Regarding Dominant Position

366. On 30 July 2009, the Uruguayan Courts[19] confirmed a resolution issued by the Antitrust Authority, which upheld the position of cable television providers by ruling that the companies which were the owners of the Uruguayan private open television channels were abusing their dominant position when they prevented cable television providers from transmitting their signals. The agency ordered the four private channels to pay the total sum of approximately USD 95,000 and instructed that they proceed to lift the prohibition.

Both the Court and the agency ruled in favour of plaintiffs on the ground of discrimination and abuse of dominant position performed precisely by the companies that owned the said Uruguayan open channels, which have been historically very important for the Uruguayan society. In this regard, the judgment stated that this discrimination had been adopted to defend selfish economic interests, and put the cable television providers in a situation that adversely affected their opportunities to compete in the market. Furthermore, the discrimination caused a significant loss to customers.

367. It is relevant to point out that the Antitrust Authority went on to ascertain that the television companies were abusing their dominant position by analysing the possibilities of establishing, by themselves, the conditions of the relevant market. The latter being obviously due to the significant part of the relevant market they shared.

368. It was not a case of essential services because the government is the Authority that grants the licences in cases of essential services, and here all the players had their own licences.

369. In Uruguayan Law, there are more subsections in section 4 dealing with group boycotts, situations that will be discussed in detail as follows.

19. Tac 2, Case N 54/2009, Ruling of 30 Jul. 2009.

II. Another Important Case on Dominant Position

370. On 10 April 2013, Uruguayan Competition Agency decided one important case involving the most important beer company in Uruguay called 'FabricasNacionales de Cerveza S.A' (FNC) which was reported by a competitor, the representative of HEINEKEN in Uruguay (Osanil SA). The latter reported FNC due to certain practices that were considered illegal.

In fact, Osanil stated that FNC: (i) prohibited small stores to sell Heineken; (ii) restricted exhibition of Heineken in supermarkets; (iii) abused of its Dominant Position, among others.

It was proved in the case that FNC offered discounts and gifts in products to small stores in exchange for limiting sales of Heineken and even for avoiding exhibition of products. This practice purported to enhance its product, beer Stella Artois. It was evidenced during the procedure that FNC during 2007 and 2008 offered a discount of 1.87% (average) to small stores to avoid selling Heineken while the ones that sold Heineken during this period received a discount of 0.96 (average).

This behaviour was considered as an abuse of the dominant position that FNC – without any doubt – has in the Uruguayan market of beers.

Considering that FNC relapsed in this type of practices, the fine that was imposed amounts to USD 1,300,000. This exemplary fine considered that this amount was around 5% of annual revenues of FNC and 1.5 times the damages caused by the anticompetitive practice.

III. Additional Case on Dominant Position

371. On *30 June 2015,* the Uruguayan Antitrust Agency decided to sanction a taxi union for punishing members who attracted clients using cell phone applications and not by the mandatory radio control equipment every unit must have. The reasoning was that even though taxi drivers must have a radio control equipment in their vehicles, the latter is not the only way in which they can attract customers, therefore being the sanctions imposed by the union a complete abuse of its dominant position, restricting the market entrance to cell phone applications that provide the same service. The union even created a new cell phone application to compete with the one introduced before. Although this situation was considered positive for consumers, who could contact taxis easily and in a less expensive way, the union continued to punish drivers who did not use the application created by it, therefore maintaining its detrimental attitude towards the market.

Considering the Taxi union relapsed in this type of practice, the fine that was imposed amounts to approximately USD 11.300.

§7. CONCENTRATIONS

In European Law, the notion of concentration[20] is laid down mainly in section 3 of Decree 139/2004. According to section 3:

> Concentration will come up when a durable change in the control occurs due to:
>
> a. merger of two or more companies or pieces of companies that used to be independent; or
> b. acquisition of a company, by one or more individuals that already controls at least one company, or by one or more companies, whereby an asset or stock deal.

372. As in the Uruguayan legal system, the purpose of identifying concentration is to identify the occurrence of a modification in the control structure of a company, since this can lead to a modification in the market structure as a whole.

373. In the US, the Herfindahl-Hirschman Index (HHI) of Concentration was created. According to Gavil,[21] a variety of units may be employed, including sales, shipments, production, capacity, or reserves – measured either in monetary or physical units. The choice of units makes a significant difference to the scenario of concentration that emerges, though the US Department of Justice & FTC Horizontal Merger Guidelines suggest circumstances wherein particular units of measurement may be the best indicator of a firm's future competitive significance.

374. This test is not applicable in Uruguay, which in this situation established a system of thresholds similar to the system originally established by section 14 of the Spanish Act 16/89 of the Competition Defence.

375. Economic concentrations typically purport to gain advantages in a market. As in the other cases discussed, concentration in itself is not illegal; the problem is the danger of allocating too much market power to only one player, who, ultimately, can fix the prices without any market control, hence adversely affecting consumers.

376. As Prof. Berdaguer[22] has maintained, it is obvious that economic concentration produces a limiting effect on competition.

377. However, as previously pointed out, an atomized market is not always possible, and consequently, monopolies in fact can be approved by the government.

20. Ortiz Blanco, *supra* n. 5, at 281.
21. Gavil, *supra* n. 14, at 480.
22. Berdaguer, *supra* n. 11, at 110.

378. To determine whether concentration has occurred, it is necessary to deal with the idea of control, which means the potential to exercise a decisive influence over the activities of another company. The idea of decisive influence is connected with the possibility that one company completely makes the decisions of another company or is at least able to block strategic decisions of the other company.

379. The Act foresees in section 7 that possible acts of economic concentration are '*those operations which suppose a variation of the control structure of the participating companies*'. Such variation could be caused by: (i) mergers; (ii) acquisition of shares, quotas or participation in companies; (iii) acquisition of ongoing concerns; (iv) total or partial acquisition of company's assets; and (v) all other kinds of legal transactions which imply the change of control of the whole or part of a concern or companies.

380. The concept of 'control' used in the Uruguayan Act refers to the question of who the decision maker is in a specific organization or group. Even though the Act does not have a definition of control for the purposes of antitrust, this idea can be derived from the context of the Act as well as from the situations the Act takes into account.

381. In the Uruguayan legal system, the General Corporate Act (16060) set forth, in section 49, the definition of 'controlled companies' by stating that a company shall be considered to be 'controlled' due to the stock ownership over it or because of special ties (e.g., when there is a contractual relation).

382. In the first case, the said act takes into account the influence the main stockholder has over the controlled company in decision-making, and in the second case, the said act takes into account the idea that a company can be controlled by another through certain contracts that allow it to exercise power over the controlled company.

383. Notwithstanding the foregoing, not all acts of economic concentration are required to be notified to the commission; the obligation to notify only exists when at least one of the two thresholds set forth by law is met. These ideas will be developed more extensively in this book when merger control is discussed.

§8. Joint Ventures

384. The concept of joint ventures is more economic than legal. Joint ventures may imply not only parties that become shareholders of a new company but also absolutely separate companies and estates that are related only pursuant to a contractual structure.

385. As a consequence, the idea of a joint venture only refers to two or more companies and/or individuals who decide to develop a common project.

386. As typically recognized, the expression 'joint venture' was originally developed in the common law systems. There is an important distinction made in the American and European legal systems between 'concentrative' joint ventures and 'cooperative' joint ventures.

387. The distinction is that in the 'cooperative' model, there is coordination among the activities of the parties in a specific business, for example, in the context of the performance of a specific contractual obligation, or in their ongoing business activity. On the contrary, the 'concentrative' joint venture implies a concentration between the parties wherein only the joint venture will operate in the market.

388. There is no distinction in Uruguayan Law between these two types of joint ventures. Moreover, joint ventures in Uruguay are typically not legal entities separate from their members (whether individuals or other legal entities).

389. In the latter distinction, it seems that the cooperative model is the one seen in the Uruguayan market but, typically, it will not be considered to be an undertaking and only the members of the joint venture will be liable. As has already been said, there is no separate legal entity in case of joint ventures and, consequently, their members are the ones to be held responsible.

390. However, a cooperative joint venture will not be prohibited as a restrictive agreement in itself. It will be considered to be a restrictive agreement if the members of the said joint venture perform anticompetitive activities. In such a case, the behaviour should be deemed to be within the purview of the events of the prohibited practices.

Chapter 5. Consequences of Violations and Enforcement Institutions

§1. Administrative Enforcement

I. The Antitrust Authorities

391. The main Authority in Antitrust Law enforcement is the *Comisión de Promoción y Defensa de la Competencia*, (Promotion and Defence of Competition Commission) (hereinafter the 'Commission' or the 'Agency') which is part of the Ministry of Economy and Finance.

392. The Commission has the power to set its own rules regarding the decision-making processes and is competent to decide, in almost all and any antitrust issues except for those reserved for the regulatory agencies in special sectors, such as the following: Communication Services' Authority (URSEC) regarding telecommunications and postal issues, URSEA regarding energy and water, and the Central Bank regarding insurance companies, brokers, and financial institutions.

393. In Resolution 1/09, the Commission briefly stated its internal rules establishing that final decisions should be adopted by at least two votes of the three members of the Commission, and also establishing the power of the disagreeing member, if any, to include his arguments in the resolution.

A. *Formation, Composition*

394. The Commission is composed of three members appointed by the head of the Executive Power from among individuals with sound professional and personal backgrounds and expertise in the area, who affirm to be independent, efficient, objective, and impartial in performing their duties.

395. The Commission members should have full-time dedication towards their duties. As an exception, they are allowed to teach and to research. The goal of the Act is to ensure the independence of the members of the Commission. To accomplish this goal, the Act does not allow the members any activities that can expose them to any situation that can affect the said independence. Teaching and researching, typically in a university, are the only activities the members are allowed, besides their work in the Commission.

396. The members are appointed for a term of six years, and once the term expires, they can be appointed again.

397. The representation of the body is exercised by the President, who has the power to act on behalf of the Commission; the presidency is, in turn, exercised for a term of two years by each of the members of the Commission.

398. The appointment of a person as a member of the Commission may be revoked by the Executive Power in the following circumstances:

(a) Negligence or unsatisfactory performance.
(b) Incapacity.
(c) Commitment of any criminal offence.
(d) Commitment of any act which may affect the name and the prestige of the Commission.

399. In the event that the appointment of a member is revoked, the new member is required to be appointed so as to complete the remaining term of the revoked appointment.

B. Investigating Powers

400. In order to perform its duties, the Commission is entitled to investigate and empowered to request from any individual or entity, public or private, any documents and/or collaboration that it may deem necessary.

401. In this regard, section 29 of Decree 404/07 states that all and any individual or entity, whether public or private, is obliged to collaborate with the Commission and to provide to it all the information and documents that the Commission may require, within a ten-day term counted from the day following the requirement by the Commission.

402. Moreover, it is stated that when the information is required of the investigated parties, non-compliance with the duty of cooperation should be interpreted as a presumption against him.

403. The duty of cooperation does not imply any obligation to reveal commercial secrets, know-how, and other protected intellectual property.

404. In any case, the information obtained by the Commission can only be used for the purpose of enabling the Commission to perform its duties.

405. In addition, the Commission is entitled to review corporate books, accounting information, and databases, minutes of board meetings and, if necessary, it can request judicial measures to be taken to collect evidence.

C. Adjudicating Powers (Ascertaining and Sanctioning)

406. In performing its role, the Commission is entitled to sanction individuals and entities, whether public or private. Sanctions may be imposed due to infringements of antitrust provisions and/or due to failure to comply with the collaboration duties regarding information and/or documents required for the investigation. This does not mean that the Commission can prosecute wrongdoers – this can be done only through the Courts – but the Commission can sanction entities or individuals, for imposing fines without a Court decision issued by a judge.

407. The Commission will only consider those cases in which either an individual or other legal entities commit a breach of the Act. The Commission does not have the power to 'adjudicate' cases as in the European system. The Act does not have a concept similar to adjudication.

408. As in the American system, the Commission has the power to investigate and sue the individuals and legal entities before a Court (such as the Antitrust Division of the Department of Justice in the US).

D. Other Institutional Tasks (Consultancy to Parliament/Government)

409. In addition to its main duties, the Commission is entitled to advise the Executive Power in relation to the promotion of competition and the policies to be adopted in this regard, as well as to suggest all the legal amendments it may deem necessary or convenient.

410. Furthermore, the Commission may issue non-binding recommendations to the Executive, the Legislative, the Judiciary, the departments (as have been defined above), and any other public entities, in relation to the treatment, protection, regulation, restriction, or promotion of competition in statutes, regulations, and administrative decisions in general.

411. Moreover, the Commission may issue non-binding recommendations in general, either referring to special sectors or to the market as a whole.

412. Finally, the Commission may provide opinions and answers to questions that any individual and/or entity may raise regarding any specific conduct and actual or eventual concentrations. In this last situation, the parties involved should be listened to, before any conclusion is reached.

II. Governmental Direct Enforcement Activities

413. Governmental enforcement activities are not only conducted through the Commission but also through the regulatory agencies that deal with special sectors such as banks (*Banco Central del Uruguay*), telecommunications and postal services (*UnidadReguladora de Servicios de Comunicaciones*), water & energy (*UnidadReguladora de Servicios de Energia y Agua*), among others.

414. Although there are certain agencies that have the particular goal of enforcing Antitrust Law, the entire system, and mainly the Judiciary, has to apply the Act as well as other related norms to defend competition.

415. A substantial part of the enforcement can be made directly by the said authorities. However, the final enforcement of fines, attachments, etc., should be left to the Judicial Power since it is deemed to be a jurisdictional task.

416. This means that the system works in a way similar to the one in the US. There are certain activities that cannot be performed by the agency, such as the enforcement of the decision punishing the individual or legal entity that breached the law. Hence, this must be conducted through the Judiciary.

417. It is similar to the situation in the US wherein the Authority builds the case and then sues before a Court to execute the decision.

III. Other Administrative Agencies Applying Antitrust Rules

418. As explained above, certain areas of activity are reserved to the regulatory agencies, such as the following: URSEC regarding telecommunications and postal services, URSEA regarding energy and water, and the Central Bank regarding insurance companies, brokers, and financial institutions.

419. It is noteworthy that the competence of these regulatory agencies extends horizontally and vertically to any market which can bring about effects under the regulated areas. In this way, the extension of its material competence becomes really important (section 27 of Act No. 18.159).

420. Typically, the authorities apply the Act, which is a comprehensive piece of legislation in terms of Antitrust Law. However, it is important to clarify that the Central Bank does have its own rules[23] which are in tune with the Act. The substantial rules are the same but have been adjusted to the specific sector, mainly in view of the banks.

IV. Administrative Fines

421. Chapter II of the Act laid down the sanctions which the Commission must apply when the administrative proceedings determine that anticompetitive practices have occurred.

422. Such sanctions can be as follows: a warning; a warning and a publication of the corresponding resolution in two newspapers; or a penalty (set between a minimum of UYU 1,00,000 and a maximum of UYU 20,000,000, 10% of the offender's annual invoice, or three times the damage caused by the anticompetitive practice, whichever is the highest).

23. Compilation of Rules of the Uruguayan Central Bank. www.BCU.gub.uy.

423. For the purpose of determining the amount of the fine, the Commission should take into account the following: the extent of the damage caused, the involvement of responsible/s, if there is a case in which more than one individual or legal entity are involved. As is obvious, in an anticompetitive practice not all participants of a scheme contribute to the same extent and this fact must be considered. The intention, the background of the infringer (i.e., if it had been involved in similar cases in the past), and the attitude assumed during the proceedings should also be considered.

424. It must be noted that in the case of prohibited practices among competitors, it will constitute a special attenuating circumstance if the person who reported the conduct was one of the participants of the said practice or if he collaborated in the gathering of evidence for the sanction of the other offenders.

425. This is similar to the 'leniency' concept of the European system. Wherein, in a situation of cartels, the participants have a limited opportunity to avoid or reduce a fine if a participant provides information about a cartel in which he has participated. In the Uruguayan system, this avoidance/reduction of the fine is not discretionary as in the case of the European Commission, which means that the benefits of voluntarily rendering information will accrue in all cases (section 34 of Decree 404/2007).

V. Administrative Injunctions and Other Restrictive Orders

426. According to section 27 of Decree 404/07, at any time in the course of an investigation, the Commission may consider the possible consequences and damage that the investigated conduct may produce, and order that the same be suspended immediately.

427. This is not an interim measure and seems to be a sort of precautionary measure. It is a specific measure that can be taken by the Authority to avoid further damage in certain special situations. The final order issued by the Authority requires that the infringer abstains from performing the activity. The order can be directly executed.

VI. Interim Measures

428. In addition to the power to order the suspension of any investigated conduct, the Commission is entitled to request the Courts to adopt any preventive measure that it may deem necessary.

429. The civil Courts are the ones with power to receive any petition relating to the adoption of preventive measures.

430. According to section 15 of Act No. 18.159, the request should be as follows: (i) based on evidence that supports the idea that there is a great risk of damage being caused if the measure is not adopted (*periculum in mora*); and (ii) presented on the grounds that the rights alleged are based on solid arguments (*bonus fumusiuris*). However, counter-guarantees are not required.

431. According to Uruguayan Law, these kind of measures typically require a guarantee to cover certain damages that the defendant can suffer in case the plaintiff loses the case. However, in such cases, the said guarantee is not required.

432. The general rules applying to preventive measures are contained in the Procedural Code, which was designed to address litigation, and therefore it was not easy to apply all its provisions to the Commission without introducing some changes. For this reason, certain special rules (such as the one that precludes counter-guarantee) are not applicable in the case of antitrust proceedings.

433. In this regard, it should be noted that ordinarily, preventive measures, which are adopted before the claim has been brought, are subject to the condition that the statement of claim is presented within the next thirty days following the adoption of the measures. If the claim is not presented within this period, the measure is lifted.

434. In the case of preventive measures adopted pursuant to a requirement of the Commission, the requirement of the initiation of claim within the term of thirty days is substituted for the initiation of the administrative proceedings.

§2. Civil Enforcement

I. Competent Civil Courts

435. The competent Courts to adjudicate on antitrust issues are the Civil Courts in Montevideo and the Courts with civil jurisdiction in the rest of Uruguay, depending on where the prohibited practice was performed. If the Commission requests a judicial measure to be adopted, these Courts will be the only ones competent to do so.

436. In principle, the trial Courts are the ones which have competence to adjudicate on an antitrust case. As in any other proceeding, both the parties can appeal against the decision, and ultimately, the decision will be taken by a Tribunal that decides in the second instance.

437. However, if a claim for damages is brought, the possibility might arise, at least theoretically, that Courts with competency limited to minor claims could be deemed competent.

II. Sanctions

A. Nullity

438. Nullity in Uruguayan Law is exceptional and, consequently, there are only certain specific cases in which nullity can be declared. There are no specific rules in the Act establishing that the consequence of a prohibited practice or any violation of antitrust rules is nullity.

439. However, section 8 of the Uruguayan Civil Code set forth that all that is made against prohibited laws is null. Consequently, it can be construed that since the Act termed anticompetitive practices as '*prohibited practices*', the agreements signed against these practices can be considered as null for civil purposes. The effect of nullity would be that the situation shall be deemed, as if the agreement had never been signed/agreed. Civil Courts are the competent bodies for the declaration of nullity.

B. Damages

440. In order to claim damages for any party, there is no need to obtain a decision of the Commission. The Courts are entitled to examine the situation independently and decide whether there has been any infringement of Antitrust Law and if so, determine if the same has caused damage or not and its entity.

441. In fact, the Uruguayan judges have the power to rule on cases wherein the cause of action is based on Antitrust Laws. Competitors, consumers, and any interested party can sue the individual or the legal entity that acted in an illegal manner.

442. Uruguay does not have specific methods to determine the amount of damage, and it will be determined in line with the general principles of civil procedure. The plaintiff should convince the judge not only regarding the case but also regarding the amount he claims.

443. As already explained in this monograph, in the Uruguayan legal system, judges are not bound by precedents. However, precedents can be used by litigators in briefings while presenting their arguments and claiming damages.

444. Finally, it is important to point out that Uruguay does not have any collective redress mechanisms (class actions) such as those in the US. If more than one individual or legal entity intends to file a class action against an undertaking, this action shall be conducted under the general principles of civil procedure.

C. Interim Measures

445. According to Articles 314.3 and 315.1 of the Procedural Code (known as 'CGP' in Uruguay), the measure can be taken without notice or intervention of the counterpart with the aim of securing the result of the action on the merits.

446. The judge has the power and the duty to do the following:

- Appreciate the necessity of the measure requested, having the power to diminish it, if considered excessive.
- Establish the reach and duration of the measure.
- Order (ex officio or upon the defendant's request) the modification, substitution, or cessation of the measure.
- Demand a counter-guarantee.
- In any case, the measures imply the plaintiff's responsibility for the damage caused to the defendant, derived from the adoption of the measure, if the final judgment is favourable to the defendant.
- Once notified, the defendant will have the opportunity to ask for the substitution or cessation of the measure affecting his assets.

447. Section 316.1 of the Procedural Code establishes the following:

> The court can order the measures that he may deem indispensable, among others, the prohibition to modify certain given situation, the preventive registration of the suit, attachment or seizure, the designation of an inspector or auditor, the intervention, or any other suitable for accomplishing the precautionary aim (Article 312).

(a) Prohibition to modify certain situation: this measure is intended to prevent the alteration of the factual or legal situation existing at the time of the measure and is taken during the term of the precautionary measure.
(b) Preventive registration of the lawsuit: this is aimed towards the publicity of the claim through the registration with the Public Registry.
(c) Attachment and Seizure: the attachment supposes the legal impossibility to dispose of goods and the seizure is the dispossession of them.
(d) Designation of an auditor, inspector, or controller: an auditor or an inspector may be designated by the court to examine, analyze, and inform, about any aspects of a company. The controller, instead, may partially or totally substitute the legal authorities of the company.

448. Uruguay is a party to the following conventions and treaties regarding emergency measures:

Inter-American Convention on Execution of Preventive Measures (1979).
Protocol on Preventive Measures of MERCOSUR (1994).

International Treaties of Montevideo on Procedural Matters of Montevideo (1940).
Treaty between Spain and Uruguay on Judicial Cooperation (1987).

449. According to the above-mentioned conventions, treaties and the CGP, the law of the state of origin determines the convenience of the measure and any objection raised before the local Court.

1. Statute of Limitations

450. Section 28 of Act No. 18.159 provides a five-year statute of limitations for actions which have their origin in prohibited practices, to be counted from the moment such conduct takes place, both regarding the Commission's powers of investigating and establishing sanctions and the rights of those who suffered damage to obtain compensation for the damage suffered. It is foreseen that the period of the statute of limitations will be interrupted by the administrative decision which orders the initiation of a procedure by the Commission ex officio, or by the decision which orders the notification of a report to the person allegedly responsible.

§3. Criminal Enforcement

I. Criminal Sanctions for Antitrust Violations

451. Uruguayan Antitrust provisions do not include criminal offences and liabilities from a criminal law standpoint. The entire approach is based on civil and administrative views and effects; hence, this chapter is not applicable to the Uruguayan system.

452. There are no criminal offences that may be considered as relevant in the antitrust context in Uruguay; it is a civil and administrative approach. For instance, in other jurisdictions, 'bid rigging' is considered a criminal offence although it does not qualify as an antitrust criminal offence in Uruguay.

453. This situation will not be considered a criminal offence in Uruguay and shall be treated in the context of 'prohibited practices', as previously discussed.

454. However, criminal enforcement is not a very important issue in Uruguay, in connection with antitrust matters, since there is not much history of antitrust in Uruguay. As a consequence, comments and jurisprudence from third countries are likely to be taken into account. However, it is worth noting that Uruguayan Antitrust Law does not contain any provision deeming any infringement a criminal offence, and the said experience and practices based on criminal case law are often not applicable.

II. Other Application of Criminal Law to Relevant Conducts

455. As already pointed out, Chapter II of the Act set out the sanctions the Commission must apply when the administrative proceedings determine that anticompetitive practices have occurred.

456. Among such sanctions is included the *adverse publicity* of the corresponding resolution in two local newspapers. Adverse publicity, along with other sanctions such as probation, is considered in modern criminal law to be a type of alternative criminal sanction that can be applicable to legal entities.

457. Although the Uruguayan legal system does not refer to criminal sanctions, following the said theory this would be a criminal sanction on one hand and the first hypothesis of a criminal sanction that can also apply to legal entities in Uruguay, on the other hand. Accepting this theory would imply an exception from the general rule, which has been applied harmoniously by Uruguayan Courts in the past, that the Uruguayan legal system does not admit the criminal liability of legal entities.

458. The question here is whether a corporation is liable for anticompetitive conduct, and if the agency applies this sanction, it is possible to claim that a criminal sanction can be imposed on a corporation or other legal entity.

459. From the civil law perspective of criminal law, only a person with a psychological point of view can commit a crime. However, the great tradition of common law has shown a different perspective. According to Lafave,[24] the early common law view was that a corporation could not be guilty of a crime: it had no mind, and thus was incapable of the criminal intent then required for all crimes; it had nobody and could not be imprisoned. This view changed with the growth and development of the corporate entity in the modern business world, and today it is almost universally conceded that a corporation may be criminally liable for actions or omissions of its agents on its behalf.

A. Alternative Sanctions

460. Fines have been, traditionally, the most favoured way to punish corporations because they have low administrative costs and bring revenue to the government treasury.

461. Even when an adequate quantum can be calculated, the eventual distribution of the burden of the fine is still an issue. A company that is slapped with a fine inevitably faces increased running costs, which are typically passed on to its consumers, shareholders, and employees.

24. Wayne R. Lafave, *Substantive Criminal Law*, vol. 2, 382 (2003).

462. The injustice becomes even more pronounced in large companies in which the shareholding interest change constantly. The individuals who are shareholders at the time of the imposition of the fine may not yet have held shares at the time the crime was committed. If these individuals had no knowledge of the crime when they bought into the company, it is difficult to pin any blame on them at all. Passing the cost of the fine on to them is therefore extremely difficult to justify.[25]

463. As a consequence of this insufficiency detected in the application of traditional sanctions against corporations, some scholars have proposed alternative sanctions such as adverse publicity.

B. Adverse Publicity

464. One alternative to imposing a fine is to cause the company to suffer from adverse publicity. This is not the publicity that is incidental to an ordinary conviction, but that which results from a formal Court-ordered sanction designed to have a punitive impact upon the corporation.

465. In the US, Courts may order a company to publicize the nature of the offence committed, the fact of conviction, the nature of the punishment imposed, and the steps that will be taken to prevent the recurrence of similar offences.[26]

466. Furthermore, in Uruguay, the adverse publicity that can be ordered by the agency can include the full resolution that condemned the antitrust offender, which can as well be deemed as a criminal sanction in the eyes of the modern theory of criminal law. Moreover, as already pointed out, since it is an alternative sanction, it can be directly imposed on the legal entity.

III. Role of Prosecutors

467. As a corollary of what was said in (a), this subsection is not applicable.

IV. Competent Criminal Courts

468. As a corollary of what was said in (a), this subsection is not applicable.

---

25. Mohan Gopalan, *Corporate Criminal Sanctions: Alternatives for the Fine City* 2 (2007).
26. Gopalan, *supra* n. 25, at 4.

Part II. The Application of the Prohibitions

Chapter 1. Restrictive Agreements

469. As already explained, as a matter of general principle, the Uruguayan Act not only prohibits the abuse of a dominant position but also any restrictive agreement that purports to restrict, limit, hinder, distort, or prevent the current and future competition in the relevant market.

470. The Act prohibits practices done as a conspiracy with others. In this situation, a competitor along with other competitors (i.e., companies or individuals) that participate in the market as different parts of production, conspire to perform restrictive acts.

471. According to Prof. Guillermo Cabanellas,[27] Argentinean legislation (and Uruguayan as well) includes within anticompetitive behaviour the ones that arise out of unilateral conduct, which is the best approach in his opinion.

472. The conduct will be considered anticompetitive regardless of the number of parties that participated in the actions that aimed to restrict the market.

The Uruguayan Competition Agency ruled in a case (*Resolution 63/2012 of 21 August 2012*), which involved two decrees of the Public Health Ministry that, allegedly, restricted healthcare companies from entering the Uruguayan medical market. Decrees 330/2010 and 008/2011 were considered illegal and consequently against Act 18,159 since it was upheld by the Agency the existence of limitation and obstacles to access into the market by new healthcare companies.

§1. Horizontal Agreements

473. Many jurisdictions have drawn the distinction between horizontal and vertical restrictions. As Cabanellas[28] stated, horizontal restrictions are the ones that occur among companies or individuals that are at the same level of the productive chain in the same market. Vertical restrictions, however, are the ones that involve companies or individuals placed at different levels of the productive chain.

27. Guillermo Cabanellas De Las Cuevas. Derecho Antimonopólico Y Defensa De La Competencia. Editorial Eliasta S.R.L., Buenos Aires (1983), 272.
28. Cabanellas, *supra* n. 27, at 271.

474. An example of the former is when the intervening parties are both manufacturers of the same product in a relevant market. Whereas, if the situation involves a manufacturer and a distributor, it is a vertical restriction.

475. Sullivan, cited by Cabanellas[29] defined vertical restrictions as the ones imposed as part of a relationship among firms that act in consecutive stages of the production and distribution of a product. If the restriction takes place through a third party that is placed in a previous or ulterior stage to the one that is suffering the restriction, it will not be deemed a vertical restriction. Moreover, if several distributors pressurize a manufacturer to establish areas of exclusivity, this restriction would be horizontal. It would be vertical if no competition existed among distributors. In another case, when connected clauses are stipulated in a contract whereby a distributor must buy products from a principal even when it does not produce them, this can affect competition.

476. Under Uruguayan Law, there is no difference between horizontal and vertical restrictions inasmuch as a prohibited practice has occurred. As a consequence, the judge adjudicating on a given case that involves a prohibited practice must analyse the latter regardless of the type of restriction.

An example of this conduct is a recent case decided by the Agency (*Resolution No. 10/2014 from 20 February 2014*) in which the owner of a clinical analysis laboratory, Mr. S denounced restrictive practices in the market of laboratories that provide such services in the city of Salto. The Agency determined the existence of an unjustified exclusion to a laboratory in a market in which the Medical – Surgical Society of Salto (the 'Society') had a relevant position and materialized the referred exclusion.

The other laboratories in the market asked the Society not to allow Mr. S' laboratory to enter into the market by not deriving patients that required clinical analysis to it. The request for not extending the quota was based on the premise that the referred situation would imply negative consequences to everyone.

The justification given by the defendants was not considered enough by the Agency that also proved the existence of a market sharing agreement entered into by the Society and other laboratories that were united in a chamber and therefore excluding the plaintiff. This agreement was considered illegal and it established an explicit clinical analysis patients derived from the Society's market allocation.

The Society had its own laboratory but pursuant to the agreement signed with clinical analysis laboratories in the market, it could not send more than 20% of the patients to it, being obliged to derive the rest to other laboratories. Once the agreement was over, this market allocation ended thus the Society was able to derive any amount of patients to its own laboratory, and therefore confirming its existence.

By virtue of the different agents' conduct a barrier for the entrance of Mr. S laboratory to the market was created, not allowing it to provide the services in which it was expert.

While it is true that not all the buyers, even those with a strong participation in the market, are obliged to buy from all the providers of a service, in this case the

29. Cabanellas, *supra* n. 27, at 271.

process of offering, the reports considered, the corporative actions of the competitors and the arguments presented in order not to assign clients to Mr. S' laboratory made de Agency conclude that it was placed an actual barrier for the entrance of said laboratory to the market. It also appears clearly established an agreement between the agents that closed the market in order to allocate it between them.

The Agency ordered to stop said practices and sanctioned five institutions with fines of approximately USD 10,600.

I. Cartels

477. In the Act, there is no definition of 'cartels'. However, an agreement among the most important producers of a good to either limit their production and/or fix prices is typically considered a cartel.

478. There are no relevant differences between the notion of cartel typically used in the European Union and in the US, in comparison with that used in the Uruguayan legal system.

479. Prof. Nuri Rodriguez[30] has said that in a cartel, particularly businessmen, maintaining their independence, agree to develop certain activities in the market in accordance with a concerted common scheme. There are several types of cartels. In certain cases, prices or selling methods are imposed on the members of the cartel. In other cases, the market is divided by granting to each member certain zones or production quotas. Furthermore, in case of a 'pool', as will be dealt with later, revenues of all members are sent to a common account to be shared among the members according to certain criteria agreed upon.

480. As already explained, according to the new Act, every possible anticompetitive case should be analysed in the light of the general principles on prohibited practices.

A. Price Fixing

481. This matter is, by far, one of the most important topics in Antitrust Law. Fixing the prices is critical for the market since it influences the quantities offered and required in a market. As a consequence, abuses in price fixing can jeopardize the market.

482. In a situation wherein a certain agent or group of economic agents perform a predatory practice, they manipulate prices – first, to eliminate competitors and second, to set prices as convenient to them and mostly against consumers' interests.

30. Nuri Rodriguez, Manual De Derecho Comercial Uruguayo, vol. 1, t. 1, Fcu (2004), 99.

1. Price Fixing in Horizontal Agreements

483. In the US, price fixing is a per se infraction, as was decided in the ruling of the *Addyston Pipe & Steel* case.[31] The prohibition includes those cases in which agents act in concert having foreseen a restriction on prices.

484. The per se approach stated in the *Addyston Pipe* case (along with the *Trans-Missouri Freight*[32] case) was clearly a hostile reaction against agreements among competitors to fix prices. However, these cases were later partially reviewed by the cases *Trenton Potteries*[33] and *Socony-Vacuum Oil.*[34] In these cases, the Supreme Court reviewed the criminal convictions, under the Sherman Act, of twenty-three producers and twenty individuals charged with fixing the prices. The argument used by the defendants was that prices *were reasonable.*

485. As Prof. Cabanellas stated,[35] the general principle that price fixing is a per se prohibition in the US should be analysed with the prevention that it may have exceptions. If the price fixing by the agent or agents is ultimately considered to be beneficial for competition, this behaviour will be deemed to be justified. However, if this exception would always be applicable, infractions under the per se rule would become rare. As a result, it is necessary to draw a distinction between those cases wherein certain conditions render unnecessary any further analysis of the effects of the behaviour under examination, and cases wherein an additional examination is not necessary.

486. It is necessary to discuss these doctrines because they are crucial in understanding the choices made by the Uruguayan system. Mainly to determine whether or not the benefit for competition is enough justification for certain practices. The short answer to this issue is 'Yes'. Uruguayan Law will deem justifiable certain practices involving prices if, ultimately, the system benefits.

487. According to Uruguayan Law, imposition of abusive prices is one of the prohibited behaviours, whether dealing with buyers or sellers. As pointed out, section 4 of the Act set forth certain practices that it deems expressly prohibited inasmuch as they coincide with any of the situations laid down in section 2.

488. The abuse in price fixing is considered, by the Uruguayan doctrine,[36] as a typical instance of abuse of dominant position. In fact, by fixing the prices, one of the parties in an agreement is enabled to do something that it could not have done in a competitive market.

---

31. *Addyston Pipe & Steel CO. v. United States*, 175 US. 211 (1899).
32. *United States v. Trans-Missouri Freight Ass'n*, 166 US. 290 (1897).
33. *United States v. Trenton Potteris Co.*, 273 US. 392 (1927).
34. *United States v. Socony-Vacuum Oil Co. Inc.*, 310 US. 150 (1940).
35. Cabanellas, *supra* n. 27, at 326.
36. Marcelo Amorin, *supra* n. 18, at 100.

489. However, the latter does not mean that price fixing can be deemed an anticompetitive practice only in the event of abuse. It can be considered an anticompetitive practice even when agreed upon by non-dominant firms. Price fixing in such a case will also be considered a prohibited practice, whether the competition and/or the consumers are harmed.

490. Section 4, paragraph A, refers to this situation when it identifies, as a prohibited conduct, the imposition, direct or indirect of prices to buy or to sell products in an abusive manner.

491. The rules in terms of price fixing would be the same for vertical or horizontal agreements. In either case, the prices resulting from a concerted scheme can be either excessive or extremely low, as part of a predatory campaign. However, the other element that should be taken into account is that the price fixing is against competition and/or the consumers.

In other countries, the fact that has to be considered is not the abuse of a dominant position but, objectively, what the price would have been in a competitive market (such as Germany). As a result, the Court in this case, to determine whether or not the price fixing is illegal, will compare the prices fixed with the corresponding price in that competitive market.

492. It is difficult to accept this method as adequate, due to the difficulties in finding a market to compare the prices fixed.

493. Cabanellas defends the illegality of these restrictive agreements alleging that if the power to set prices was taken from the government legal Authority, it was not in order to give the said power to manufacturers.

494. Nevertheless, as the US case law is typically taken into account by lawmakers and commentators while reviewing Antitrust Law, it is relevant to briefly discuss that this issue was recently raised in the US in the *Leggin Creative Eláter Products*[37] case of 2007. In this case, the Supreme Court overruled a former precedent (*Dr Miles* case of 1911) in which it was decided that the imposition of resale price is not illegal. Throughout history, and after the *Dr Miles* case in the US, vertical price fixing was deemed illegal. However, the Court in the 2007 case reviewed the precedent, and based its ruling on the 'rule of reason'. According to this new standard, the Court should examine, by considering each particular case, whether the vertical price-fixing can adversely affect competition.

495. Even though the last ruling of the Supreme Court has been largely criticized by a certain sector of the American doctrine, others have been more supportive, and accepted this split of Authority as beneficial to the system. In this sense, Prof. Thomas Arthur[38] wrote about the new Authority as follows.

37. *Leggin Creative Eláter Products v. United States*, 127 S. Ct. 2705 (2007).
38. Thomas C. Arthur, 62 Smu L. Rev. 387 (2009).

496. This decision has been sharply criticized both since it strayed from basic antitrust principles and since it overruled a precedent that has been widely relied upon for nearly a century. These criticisms are misplaced. The 'per se' rule in *Dr Miles* was not based on core antitrust principles, and the Court has permitted it to be evaded over most of its history.

497. In closing, under Uruguayan Law, the limit of price fixing is typically the abuse of the party that has a dominant position. For instance, if a group of agents of the market decide to fix the prices horizontally and the emerging price is beneficial for consumers (and it is not a predatory scheme), a Uruguayan Court will typically not see a case of abuse under the said circumstances.

498. On the contrary, if the price is not beneficial to consumers, and there is an abuse in the price fixing, a judge will consider it a prohibited practice.

499. If the participants to the agreement set a monopolistic price, but none of them is independently a dominant agent, the price fixing will be typically considered to be prohibited if it affects consumers or competition.

In a recent case (*Resolution No. 72/2012 of 21 September 2012*) the Uruguayan Competition Agency decided in an action brought against an organization of shipping agents (CENNAVE) which set a tariff for the services rendered by its affiliates. In the context of the proceeding, it was alleged that the tariff was only a guideline which was not mandatory for members. However, it was proved in the proceeding that during many years all the members of the association followed the same tariff and considered it as mandatory. Since the Agency deemed that the tariff affected the market and consequently that the price fixing was anticompetitive. One feature of the case that was considered critical was that the referred tariff was used to increase the prices of the services ultimately damaging the consumers. This was deemed as abusive since performed by an organization that had a dominant position. The Uruguayan Agency highlighted the fact that no argument was made in favour of a possible contribution to the efficiency of the system.

500. In the Uruguayan doctrine, Prof. Olivera García[39] has maintained that in Uruguay, price fixing will mostly be related to an abuse of a dominant position. Although in most of the world's legal systems price fixing is considered anticompetitive per se regardless of the reasons or motives behind it, in Uruguay it is only illegal if performed abusively.

501. However, in the authors' opinion, it is not indispensable an 'abusive' scenario to consider that we are dealing with price fixing as an illegal practice. In fact, it is plausible that an anticompetitive practice performed by a non-dominant firm ultimately affects competitors and/or competition.

39. Ricardo Olivera García, *Introducción al Derecho de la Competencia*, Nuevo Régimen de Derecho de la Competencia, UM (2001), 30.

502. Because the new Act is rather recent, there are few cases related to price fixing that have been decided under the Act. Nevertheless, when the former Act was in force (with similar principles on this regard) the jurisprudence of the Antitrust Agency was consistent, and it decided in favour of these clauses that included price fixing by manufacturers.

503. In Uruguay, the said position of the Antitrust Agency supported by the majority of the Uruguayan doctrine has made clauses containing price-fixing rather common in the Uruguayan market.

An example of this antitrust behaviour is a case (*Resolution No. 80/014 of 19 August 2014*) recently decided by the Agency in which it was proved that local companies devoted to the distribution and sale of frozen food were establishing mandatory minimum retail prices. The practice was conducted by distributors, who obliged different shops and stores to sell their products to general public with certain minimum prices. This behaviour was accompanied by an extremely strict control and sanction system, consisting of cutting the deliveries of the distributed products to the facilities that did not follow their guidelines. Moreover, the practice was also performed by a very popular supermarket chain that pressed frozen food distributors in order to make them impose to other supermarkets or stores minimum retail prices, punishing them for breaches by not buying their products or not putting them on display for sale. The agency did not consider that the conducts were justified or had a beneficial impact for consumers; therefore, it sanctioned the companies involved with substantial fines of USD 218,000 and USD 18,000 approximately.

A similar situation occurred in the case resolved by the Agency by Resolution N°158/016, in which the referred public entity punished several television brands, for the fixing of minimum retail prices for the stores that sold their products. This redounds in an increase in the prices the general public have to pay for the products, since stores cannot set lower prices to compete with each other.

B. Market/Client Allocation

504. Price fixing is not the only way to affect competition, because by dividing markets, competitors can achieve an illegal monopoly or oligopoly. Market division can be reached geographically by agreeing not to compete in certain areas, or by assigning customers or categories of customers. In accordance with this kind of covenants, competitors agree not to solicit each other's customers.

505. Section 4, paragraph H of the Uruguayan Act lays down rules regarding unjustifiable market allocation, to prevent certain agents from entering a specific market. This is done by granting exclusivity and, as a consequence, restricting operations of the other competitors.

506. This illegal practice is performed through agreements among competitors whereby they divide the market into zones or concert activities by coordinating the products that each member of the group will manufacture or sell. Likewise, they divide the services the group's members will render, preventing, in all of the cases mentioned, other competitors from participating in a specific zone.

507. These agreements are directly against consumers' interests since they will not only have only one option to acquire a specific product or receive a service but also have to pay a higher price than the one in a competitive market.

508. As Prof. Caffera[40] has said, it is a bilateral contract in which both parties promise to refrain from doing business in a specific zone.

509. In Uruguay, market allocation is not a per se prohibited conduct, since to be deemed illegal the practice is required to have been performed unjustifiably. This means that the market allocation can be deemed legal if it is based on commercial reasons.

An important case on market/client allocation was one decided by the Agency in April 2014 (*Resolution No. 24/2014 dated 1 April 2014*). A group of companies from the market of processed products derived from tomatoes (tomato juice, sauce, puree, etc.) formed a cartel by which they avoided competition, sharing each other's participation fees.

The group of companies engaged the services of a printing company in order to prepare their different products' packaging on the grounds it quoted a minor price because of the volume of work to do.

The Agency did not find any reasonable and convincing argument to justify this practice; on the contrary it discovered a close relationship between the cartel companies that shared a fluid and constant exchange of information. Furthermore, the Agency could not find a difference in the price the printing company charged for its work, resulting in no variations per amount of boxes sent, the price for each company was the same before, during and after the agreement. Thus the Agency concluded there was a market sharing agreement between the companies and quoting of production. The little or no competence in the referred market lead the Agency to such conclusion, once the agreement terminated prices increased, which was a sign of a more competitive market.

It was also proved the existence of control among the participants of the compliance of the agreement's terms and sanctions to those who did not follow its guidelines.

The cartel companies' behaviour distorted the market by deviating it from free competition's rules. The agreement and Constitution of the cartel had an uncompetitive objective and effect.

The Agency ordered the companies to stop the information exchange, price fixing, market/client allocation, and any other conduct that could affect the market and competition. Cartel companies were sanctioned with fines, the highest of them was of approximately USD 430,000.

40. Caffera, *supra* n. 17, at 577.

C. Production/Innovation Limitation

510. Section 4, paragraph B lays down certain kinds of conduct that are considered to be against the law, since they have the potential to ultimately affect the competitors. Not only are absolute restrictions included but also partial restrictions. Likewise, the provision covers unilateral and concerted conduct among agents of the market.

511. Moreover, not only should abuse of dominant position be considered in this case but also unilateral conduct.

512. The Uruguayan Act deems as unfair any commercial practices that limit, restrict, or set volumes of production or distribution against consumers' interests.

513. This is clearly the situation wherein competitors agree to sell in the market a limited volume of products, less than the full productive capacity, in order to restrict the offer and, consequently, to obtain a higher price for the product and gain better revenues.

514. Another situation, which can be cited as being within the scope of this section, is when an agent or group of agents destroys or stores raw materials or final products to create a shortage of supply in the market, in order to later gain a higher price for the scant product.

515. Furthermore, the same subsection (B) of section 4 deems the following as illegal conduct: purporting to limit the technological development of products, services, or productive structures.

516. Uruguayan Law considers that the above conduct negatively affects a more effective production which, ultimately, will harm customers and consumers, since technological development is made to produce better and cheaper products, and this objective cannot be accomplished in the above scenario.

517. As in other cases, section 4 sets out that to be deemed as illegal, the scheme in question should be unjustifiable. To be considered 'unjustifiable', the scheme should not have any reasonable commercial bases. As a result, provided it is possible to prove that the measure taken has a reasonable explanation that will benefit consumers, it will not be considered illegal.

D. Group Boycott

518. This is the situation wherein a concerted group of agents refuses to sell a product or to render a service to a specific company or individual.

519. Group boycott is also widely referred to as 'concerted refusals to deal'. It has also been considered as a 'per se infraction' in the US. A group boycott is a product of collusion in the sense of agreement.[41] The collusive group boycotts the ones that directly restrict output or raise prices.

520. There are instances of group boycotts in situations wherein a group of suppliers collude, in order to coerce acceptance of a lower price than the one that can be reasonably charged in a competitive market.

521. There are cases in which a group of sellers force the buyer(s) to accept the price or simply refuse to deal with the buyer(s). Such situations lead to anticompetitive prices which are beyond the market rationale.

522. Another type of boycotts is the exclusionary type. These are typically performed by competitors by raising the costs of rivals' products, obstructing the rival's ability to expand or enter into a market, limiting its access to a needed source of supply or to customers, among others.

1. Restrictive Measures Preventing New Competitors: Section 4, Subsection (F)–Essential Facilities

523. The Act lays down that it is illegal to prevent competitors from accessing infrastructures that are essential for the production, distribution, or commercialization of products, services, or productive infrastructure.

524. 'Essential infrastructure' implies those facilities which are necessary for competitors to develop their activities and consequently, restrict the possibility of gaining new customers.

525. A clear example of a restrictive measure purporting to prevent new competitors can be found when a new telecommunications company or a railroad company wants to establish itself in a market. These companies, to be profitable, need to use the already built infrastructure since the prospect of assembling a new railroad track or a new antenna net in the same market will make the investment absolutely non-feasible for the new competitor.

526. Those agents in the market who already control the essential facilities when the new investor wants to establish himself in this new market will clearly have a dominant position or even a monopoly.

527. This Uruguayan provision was conceived under the traditional American doctrine of 'essential facilities' which has a long history in the US. Its origin can be traced back to the *Terminal Railroad* case[42] of the Supreme Court in 1912. After that decision, the Courts in the US consistently applied the 'essential facilities' doctrine.

41. Gavil, *supra* n. 14, at 127.
42. *United States v. Terminal Railroad Ass'n*, 224 u. s. 383 (1912).

In sum, the said American doctrine implies that the general rule that a company has no obligation to deal with its rivals has certain exceptions.

528. In general, it is true that a company can refuse to deal with its competitors. But that right is not unlimited; it exists only if there are justified competitive reasons for the refusal. The right to refuse to deal is 'neither absolute nor exempt from regulation'.[43]

529. The 'essential facility' doctrine has also been considered as another case of 'refusal to deal', a matter that will be discussed in this book. They are cases in which a firm that has a dominant position or a monopoly excludes current or potential competitors from the market.

530. The 'essential facilities' doctrine imposes liability when one company that has control over an essential facility prevents a second company from accessing a product or service that the second company must obtain in order to compete with the first one.

531. In Uruguay, another situation that has been included in this subsection is when consumers are denied access to a distribution channel, for example, when a competitor is not allowed to use the facilities of a harbour.

532. Ultimately, the goal of these rules is to foster competition in a relevant market.

533. In those situations wherein essential facilities are under the state's control (state's monopoly), if a competitor is denied access to a certain essential facility, this denial will be deemed legal under section 2, subsection 4 of the Act in Uruguayan Law.

534. Notwithstanding cases in which the state is involved, for the rest of the cases, the Uruguayan doctrine[44] has considered the application of the 'essential facilities' doctrine as an exception to the general regime in which any individual is free to decide whether or not he wants to enter into an agreement with another. In such a case, the lawmaker forces individuals to make this deal.

535. However, other commentators[45] have maintained that the owners of the essential facilities always have the right of a price for the use of them. The agents who want to use the facilities should pay for the use.

---

43. *Lorain Journal co. v. United States*, 342 u. s. 143, 155 (1951).
44. Caffera *supra* n. 17, at 591.
45. Paula Algorta Morales, *Prácticas Prohibidas*, Estudios sobre Defensa de la Competencia y Relaciones de Consumo, Fcu, Montevideo (2008), 49.

536. For this reason, the doctrine of essential facilities has been criticized as a non-feasible way of preventing abuse of dominant position. In the case of the railroad company that wants to establish a branch in a certain country, even when it is legal to force the owner of the railroad track to rent it to the new company for a price, it would be difficult to control the conditions.

537. It may be that the owner of the essential facility wishes to release the use of the railroad track in a period compatible with its schedule and that the hours then available to the other company to use the track may make the investment non-feasible. Another possibility is that the owner of the railroad track is the state, which can distribute the hours and organize the schedule in a fair manner. This is the situation in Uruguay.

538. Nevertheless, we can extend this hypothesis to the case of the antennas for a technological company.

2. Unjustifiably Hinder the Access to a Market of Potential Competitors: Section 4, Subsection G

539. This is a typical situation among competitors or between suppliers and distributors purporting to prevent new economic agents from entering the market.

540. This practice is typically related to other anticompetitive situations (e.g., exclusivity agreements among competitors).

541. Nevertheless, as can be observed, the Act says that to be deemed illegal, the practice must be performed unjustifiably. For instance, as Prof. Martinez Blanco[46] wrote, hindering access to the market may be justified by the exercise of intellectual property rights. In such cases, the owner of the intellectual property right has the opportunity to use the power typically during a period of time when denying replication to competitors.

542. In such cases, overlapping interests and norms are to be dealt with. A couple of essential rights arise. On the one hand, we have the anticompetitive conduct whereby an agent exclusively uses a patent that other competitors wish to use, and on the other hand, it is clear that the legal system needs to protect the inventor/patent holder, so as to foster new inventions.

543. However, the test under Uruguayan Law, in this case, would be the presence of abuse. In this case, the abuse can be found in cases wherein the patent holder uses the patent in an unfair manner. For example, the abusive price fixing in medicines is typically considered to be an abusive use of intellectual property rights.

---

46. Camilo Martinez Blanco, Manual Basico De Derecho De La Competencia, FCU (2008), 147.

544. If an individual or company holds a dominant position in a relevant market, it possesses a privilege but there are limits. If the said rights are used in an abusive way, they will be considered to be anti-competitive.

E. Collusion on Other Objects

545. Other situations of collusion are laid down in section 4, paragraph C of the Act, such as when it is unjustifiably applied to third parties unequal commercial conditions in cases of equivalent transactions, placing one agent at a disadvantage before the rest of the group.

546. In such a case of collusion, discrimination is the issue. Herein, a group of agents of the market offer different and inconvenient conditions to a specific individual or company in order to exclude it from the relevant market.

547. This is typical among agents placed at different levels of the productive process (e.g., suppliers and distributors). This prohibited practice can be performed by buyers or sellers who hold an important power over a relevant market, and who can impose different and unequal conditions based on these circumstances.

548. For instance, there may be a group of suppliers that has many distributors in a relevant market, and they begin, in a coordinated manner, to unjustifiably impose unfair conditions on one distributor. Under these circumstances, the latter cannot compete in the market in the same egalitarian conditions with the rest of the distributors.

549. This case of discrimination can be found in different factors such as price, term, modes of delivery, credit benefits, among others.

550. As already pointed out, in order to be considered illegal, the practice should be commercially unjustified and place the harmed economic agent in a position of discrimination and disadvantage before the rest of the competitors.

551. Likewise, this general principle needs to be deemed in Uruguay in view of its peculiar 'rule of reason'. The fact that a company simply demands more prices or gives less credit benefits to an agent, does not per se amount to anticompetitive behaviour. To be deemed against the Antitrust Law, the unequal conditions must be unjustified. Moreover, it is required to have a disadvantageous effect when compared with competitors.

552. As already explained, Uruguay is a '*rule of reason*' country (with the peculiarities discussed) and to determine whether or not a certain practice is prohibited, it is necessary to analyse it in the light of the principles and specific cases set out by law.

553. As already explained, cooperation agreements are not, in themselves, anti-competitive. However, section 4 paragraph E provides for a situation in which a cooperative agreement is deemed illegal.

554. This is the situation when two or more economic agents enter into agreements whereby they coordinate either submission or abstention in private or public bids.

555. This practice occurs when competitors coordinate their behaviour either by agreeing upon prices and ways in which services will be rendered, dividing territorial zones, etc. or when competitors agree not to submit their proposals in a coordinated manner.

556. By preventing concerted presentations, the law intends to prevent the situation wherein the company seeking bidders has to choose from among the proposals the competitors had mutually agreed to submit, which, in general, will disadvantage the first cited agent.

557. For instance, the bidders can agree to submit only one proposal in each case making competition among them impossible.

558. Whereas, by avoiding concerted abstentions, the law aims to prevent the situation wherein the company asking for proposals should have to restructure the offer by providing better conditions to the bidders.

II. Information Exchange Practices

559. The Uruguayan legal system does not provide rules regarding the sharing of information among competitors being a specific prohibited practice.

560. This situation has a long tradition in the European Union, and it was considered anticompetitive. Information exchanges can happen by the sharing of data among competitors. This information exchanged can involve information about sales, prices, rebates, customers, production costs, capacities, and information regarding marketing.

561. In Uruguay, this practice would be considered illegal only if it is viewed in combination with some of the prohibited practices already discussed in this book. In fact, not only is there no provision condemning the sharing of information among competitors, but it is also common to find agreements in which parties agree to exchange information about the market, clients, etc.

562. The test of this kind of practice will always be the consumer and the market in its entirety. For instance, if two competitors exchange information with the objective of setting abusive prices, this would be considered anticompetitive. However, the sole act of sharing information is not illegal in itself.

563. On the contrary, in Argentina, sharing information with competitors under certain conditions is deemed illegal. In fact, Article 47 subsection K of the Argentinean law provides that concerted practices among competitors based on information exchange are not allowed.

III. Cooperation Agreements

A. Research and Development

564. In the US, a cooperative research and development agreement is typically defined as an agreement between a government agency and a private company to work together on research and development.

565. There is no such agreement defined in the Uruguayan legal system.

B. Specialization

566. This concept is not relevant under Uruguayan Antitrust Law.

C. Standardization

567. This concept is not relevant under Uruguayan Antitrust Law.

D. Joint Production

568. This concept is not relevant under Uruguayan Antitrust Law, inasmuch as a prohibited practice or abuse of a dominant position is not being dealt with as well. Joint production, as a sole concept, is not a prohibited practice as viewed by Uruguayan Antitrust Law.

E. Joint Purchasing

569. This concept is not relevant under Uruguayan Antitrust Law, inasmuch as a prohibited practice or abuse of a dominant position is not being dealt with as well. Joint purchasing, as a sole concept, is not a prohibited practice as viewed by Uruguayan Antitrust Law.

F. Joint Selling

570. This concept is not relevant under the Uruguayan Antitrust Law, inasmuch as a prohibited practice or abuse of a dominant position is not being dealt with as well. Joint selling, as a sole concept, is not a prohibited practice as viewed by Uruguayan Antitrust Law.

§2. VERTICAL AGREEMENTS

I. Distribution

571. A distribution agreement is used when one party that acts as a distributor sells the products or goods of the other party (principal or supplier) in a specified territory. In Uruguay, distribution can be either exclusive or non-exclusive, being considered exclusivity, by the Uruguayan doctrine, as a feature that can be disregarded in a distributorship (i.e., exclusivity is not essential).

572. The products to be distributed are purchased from the principal and can only be sold within the said specified territory.

573. The model of the distribution agreement has been used to provide the hypothesis in different parts of this monograph, due to the fact that many antitrust issues are raised in the context of distributorships, showing the link between distribution agreements and Antitrust Law.

A. Exclusive Distributorship

574. Exclusivity is not the essence of a distribution agreement, but in spite of the non-essential feature of this element, agreements usually include it. Exclusivity is not the rule under the Uruguayan system (it is not implied); consequently, it is necessary to stipulate it in the distribution contract.

575. If exclusivity was not specifically stipulated, the agreement will be considered as a non-exclusive one. As a consequence, the supplier will be able to appoint other distributors to sell the products.

576. In an exclusive distributorship, the supplier and the distributor agree that the latter will deal exclusively with the supplier for certain products in a specific territory. This kind of agreement prevents the supplier's competitors from gaining access to the market due to the exclusive distribution network organized by the supplier.

577. In general, Antitrust Law across the world has been qualified as restrictions between non-competitors (vertical restrictions). In the US, since 1977, the Courts have consistently upheld the position that exclusive distributorships are not per se prohibited. However, the arrangement will be in violation of Antitrust Law if it may substantially affect inter-brand competition or if it is trying to create a monopoly.

578. More than one factor should be taken into account in determining whether an exclusive distributorship is against the law. For instance, if the supplier has a substantially dominant position to unreasonably restrain business in a relevant market, by raising prices beyond the competitive level, it will be considered unlawful in the US.

579. Notwithstanding the foregoing, in some cases exclusive distribution may be against the Antitrust Laws. An example from the American system is the recent *Dentsply*[47] case in which a leading manufacturer of false teeth was sued by the Justice Department in Delaware for unlawfully maintaining its monopoly power by entering into exclusive distributor agreements with most of the nation's tooth distributors. The plaintiff said that the defendant had maintained a 70% share of the artificial tooth market for over ten years, and had tried to restrict competition by depriving its rivals of effective distribution by entering into exclusive distributor agreements. The case is still pending.

580. Exclusive distributorships are commitments made by a supplier not to appoint more than one or a limited number of dealers within a specific geographical area. As Gavil[48] says, by limiting the number of dealers that might directly compete with each other in the sale of the same line of products, exclusive distributorships limit inter-brand competition, exactly like territorial and customer restraints. The cited author maintains that exclusive distributorships are 'ubiquitous and rarely present any serious antitrust concerns'.

581. In Uruguay, exclusivity in distributorships is not deemed illegal inasmuch as it does not affect the relevant market by coinciding with any of the prohibited practices already discussed.

582. In fact, section 4 subsection G of the Act, as analysed, lays down that it is a prohibited practice to unjustifiably hinder the competitors' access to the market.

583. Upon closer examination, it seems evident that through exclusive distributorship, competitors are being prevented from accessing the marketplace. However, as mentioned, and following the trend of the American case law, exclusivity in distribution agreements is allowed in Uruguay as long as it does not illegally prevent competitors from entering into the market and consequently affect consumers.

584. Provided exclusivity is agreed upon with a distributor, and there are more distributors who are able to sell competitors' products, the clause will be legal and enforceable. Nevertheless, if the supplier were to organize an exclusive distributor

47. *United States v. Dentsply International*, Inc. 277 F. Supp. 2d 387 D. Del. (2003).
48. Gavil, *supra* n. 14.

network that made it impossible for other competitors to participate in the marketplace even when they attempted to do so, then under these circumstances, the exclusive agreement will be deemed unlawful under Uruguayan Law.

B. Exclusive Dealing

585. Exclusive dealing agreements are not specifically regulated in the Uruguayan legal system. They are agreements in which one party promises to deal exclusively with another and, thus, not to deal with competitors of the other party. Such agreements can raise several issues under Antitrust Law because, by denying competitors the access to the goods or services offered by a competitor, they can remove this competitor from the marketplace or jeopardize the latter's ability to compete.

586. This kind of agreement can be considered 'exclusionary behaviour' because it can eliminate competitors.

587. In the US, exclusive dealing is not illegal conduct per se. It is governed by Antitrust Law since it can cause the eviction of competitors from an important share of the affected marketplace.

588. To determine if a particular exclusive arrangement can be considered an illegal restraint on freedom of trade, Courts in the US apply the 'rule of reason' upheld in the *Board of Trade of the City of Chicago* case[49] in which the Court stated the following:

> The true test of legality is whether the restraint imposed is such as merely regulates and perhaps thereby promotes competition or whether it is such as may suppress or even destroy competition. To determine that question the Court must ordinarily consider the facts peculiar to the business to which the restraint is applied; its condition before and after the restraint was imposed; the nature of the restraint and its effect, actual or probable. The history of the restraint, the evil believed to exist, the reason for adopting the particular remedy, the purpose or end sought to be attained, are all relevant facts.

589. In Uruguay, as a matter of principle, exclusive dealing is not considered illegal per se. Some practices can be considered unlawful and against Antitrust Law inasmuch as they are also against some of the prohibited practices laid down in the Uruguayan Act. In essence, they will be considered illegal if by selling products exclusively to a particular company, the manufacturer or supplier intends to exclude other competitors.

---

49. *Board of Trade of City of Chicago v. United States*, 246 US. 231 (1918).

590. At the end of the day, what is important to Uruguayan Law is that consumers are not adversely affected by any competitor that is strategizing in the market in order to exercise maximum control over it. This is the kind of behaviour that Uruguayan Law and Antitrust Laws across the world are trying to rule out from the market.

591. An example of this antitrust behaviour is a case (Resolution N°22/016) recently decided by the Antitrust Authority. In this case the most important national beer producer, abusing its dominant position, executed exclusive dealing agreements with the stores that sold their products, thus affecting the competition by avoiding other beer producers or importers to sell their products in the same stores. The Authority did not find, due to the structure of the relevant market, efficiency arguments to explain the exclusive dealing agreements, and therefore considered the latter to be anticompetitive. This vertical restriction could act as an obstacle to the entrance to the market of other competitors and to the expansion of competitors.

C. Selective Distribution

592. Selective distribution is a concept highly developed in the European Union, but not in the Uruguayan system, as a separate category of prohibited practices. In fact, under Uruguayan Law, being selective, in terms of to whom to deal with, is deemed a legal practice.

593. Distributing products only to those companies or retailers who agree to sell the products for no less than a certain price, who accept minimum turnovers, or who meet other specific requirements stipulated by the supplier, is not illegal in Uruguay. Furthermore, this is quite common in the Uruguayan market. It is clear that in the Uruguayan system, the supplier is in a better position to negotiate than the distributor.

594. The supplier is in a better position and if there is an abuse of it, it will amount to anticompetitive conduct. It is not that Uruguayan Law is presuming that a dominant position is held by the supplier but, in practice, suppliers have the opportunity to sell their products to various distributors. This is a non-egalitarian relationship, in terms of negotiation.

595. However, the mere fact of negotiating with the other party, knowing that the supplier is in a better position, is not a per se prohibited practice. By categorizing certain terms as deal-breakers, the supplier is not performing an anticompetitive conduct. As a consequence, it is possible that if a certain distributor is not amenable to sign the contract, the supplier will negotiate with a different distributor.

596. In Europe, selective distribution is used primarily for goods such as stereo equipment or furniture. This technique allows suppliers to avoid price competition and maintain more control over the way their products are sold.

597. As Prof. Bortolotti[50] pointed out, through selective distribution contracts a producer establishes a preferential relationship with a number of retail outlets, selected on the basis of such characteristics as the producer considers necessary for the optimal sale of his products. This type of agreement is used especially when the producer wishes to have a direct control over the way his products are distributed by retailers. This is particularly the case with respect to high technology products and luxury products (which must maintain a certain image which can be warranted only if they are sold in shops of a certain standard). Since the purpose of a selective network is that the products are sold only in the selected outlets, the establishment of such a network, by its very nature, implies that the members of the network must undertake not to sell the products to traders who do not belong to the selective distribution network. This is the main issue which gives rise to a possible conflict with the rules of competition, as will be seen hereafter.

598. The fact that selective distribution is typically used simultaneously by several competing suppliers is a fundamental difference with respect to franchising, which normally implies the obligation to sell only the franchisor's brand.

599. In sum, it can be said that selective distribution is employed to ensure that products are sold in a specific territory in the same conditions and in the market that is considered best for selling the product in question.

1. Vertical Price Fixing

600. Vertical price fixing is the one affecting agents placed at different levels in the productivity chain. This type of vertical action is taken in connection with the division of the economic process in different and subsequent stages. This situation brings, as a natural consequence, a situation wherein an agent placed in a lower level of the productive chain may exercise a certain amount of influence over a superior market player. Moreover, if the price fixing is abusive and affects the relevant market, the practice will be considered to be prohibited by the Uruguayan Act.

601. Section 2 of the Act does not distinguish between horizontal and vertical agreements. Moreover, section 2 classifies as prohibited practices, any conduct, or recommendations which aim to restrict, limit, hinder, distort, or prevent competition.

602. In principle, price fixing is deemed to be a prohibited practice due to the effects it has over the independence of the parties who accept the recommendation or perform their part in the agreement.

603. However, several arguments have been raised in Uruguay to uphold the admissibility of this kind of price fixing. There are commercial reasons that can justify the action. One of the most important arguments used by the scholars that have

50. Bortolotti, *supra* n. 41.

admitted this practice is the protection of the brand, since setting a price too low would make the customers interpret it as a bad product.

604. If the manufacturer is prevented from fixing or recommending reasonable prices to distributors, two adverse consequences, from the manufacturer's point of view, may arise, as follows:

(1) the above-mentioned fact that when one distributor sets a price very low, it can adversely affect the brand and the prestige of the manufacturer; and
(2) it is natural that manufacturers expect their products to be sold in the market at one uniform price or at least without significant differences in the price.

605. The said arguments have been rebutted with the argument that if the price is increased due to an artificial price-fixing done by a distributor, this will be far from being beneficial to consumers.

606. Moreover, in cases of vertical price fixing, although there is a split of Authority in Uruguay, recommended prices are, in general, allowed. As previously stated, the test will be the abuse of a dominant position. However, if a manufacturer can commercially justify the price suggestion or even, under certain circumstances, the price fixing, for example, the protection of the brand, or the benefit of consumers, an Uruguayan Court will typically uphold the clause.

D. Franchising

607. According to Uruguayan Law, 'franchise' is an agreement that is generally considered by the Uruguayan doctrine to be a mode of distribution like agency or distribution agreements. However, there is a new tendency to consider the franchise agreement to be one of the technology transfer agreements.

608. Beyond the different opinions on this agreement, it is a fact that the franchise is, for most companies in the world, a useful vehicle to enter into foreign markets. Furthermore, the Uruguayan and Argentinean doctrines do not have a uniform definition of franchising, and scholars have not yet achieved a consensus either on the characteristics or on elements that comprise the idea of 'franchise'.

609. For instance, Professor *Marzorati*[51] belongs to the group of scholars that considers the franchise 'as a method or system of distribution of products or services'.

51. Osvaldo Marzorati, *Franchising* 1 (Astrea 2001).

610. In commercial relationships, the Franchisor has a product or service which has been tested in the market and also has a system to develop his business successfully. Moreover, the Franchisor is interested in gaining quick access to other markets (national or international), where his product is not well known.

611. On the other side of the commercial relationship is the investor (the Franchisee), who has the money to invest in a new business, but attempts to avoid, as far as he can, the risks related to business. In general, this is the main reason considered by investors when they consider a franchise agreement, because through this system, which has already been tried and proven successful in some markets of the world, investors receive a low-risk business.

612. According to Professor *Nelson*,[52] the term 'franchise' is among the least well-defined of all business relationships, probably second only to the 'joint venture' in this respect.

613. Franchise agreements contain, in variable proportions, elements of distribution and licensing agreements. As generally understood, the term refers to a relationship involving the sale by the Franchisor of goods or services using trade names, trademarks and other distinctive symbols, as well as, in some cases, a patented or unpatented invention, formula or know-how, provided by the franchisor.

614. This type of agreement, which is one of the best-developed agreements in the US is not regulated under Uruguayan Law.

615. All aspects regarding this agreement are regulated by the parties. In general terms, it is possible to note that Uruguay has only a small amount of legislation that refers to distribution agreements in general, as agreements which are governed by general law principles applicable to all kind of contracts.

616. Franchisors typically have substantial market power, and a dominant position that implies the power of raising and maintaining prices above a competitive level. The law does not presume that a dominant position is held by the supplier and, consequently, there is no prerequisite for the prohibition to apply. In fact, we are considering a practical scenario in which the weight – in terms of negotiation – the franchisor has is more important than the franchisee. As explained, when considering distribution agreements, in dealings with franchisees, franchisors have a better position to negotiate the terms of the agreement. This power may arise from the franchisee's interest in obtaining the investment.

617. Abuse of this power can affect competition and ultimately harm the final consumers, the public. In Uruguay, it is considered as a legal practice that franchisors require the franchisee to buy a specific product from a particular seller. For instance, in the case of McDonald's – even though it is not a franchise in Uruguay

52. Steven Nelson, *Negotiating and Drafting Agency, Distribution and Franchise Agreements*, ABA, Sec. Intl. L. & Prac. (1992).

anymore – it is possible to ensure that the French fries are bought from a seller established by the franchisor, which may confirm the uniformity and quality of franchise offerings, maintaining or enhancing the goodwill of the system.

618. Notwithstanding the foregoing, this simple situation can be deemed illegal if the franchisor's imposition of the above requirement involves abuse of a dominant position, since the conduct can be considered to be within the purview of the 'prohibited practices' laid down in section 4 as discussed.

619. There is no doubt regarding the influence the franchisor exercises over the franchisee, which may lead to an abuse of the dominant position, which is illegal in Uruguay. However, if the franchisor does not reach the point of abuse, the conduct will be considered legal, even when he is clearly directing the franchisee to certain vendors, who are not the best option in terms of prices. The latter will not be deemed as illegal in Uruguay.

620. Another situation typically seen in franchise agreements, such as the exchange of information regarding clients and suppliers, is not deemed illegal, since such information is considered to be part of the necessary information both parties need to have to structure the commercial relationship. From the franchisor's point of view, knowing the levels of sales, the type of clients, the best month of the year in terms of selling, among others, is critical in determining whether or not to appoint other franchisees to cover other territories in the country.

621. It is important to clarify that the so-called disclosure laws, very well known in the US and in Europe, and not regulated under Uruguayan Law, are not being referred to here.

II. Technology Licensing

A. *Patent Licensing*

622. In Uruguay, there is no specific rule about the effects of Licensing of Intellectual Property in Antitrust Law.

623. However, as previously stated, every conduct has the potential to be considered anticompetitive if it can be connected with any of the prohibited practices mentioned in section 4 of the Act.

624. For this reason, it is important to review the Antitrust Guidelines for the Licensing of Intellectual Property of the United States, as the Uruguayan Law regarding intellectual property is similar to the laws in force in the US.

625. The US passed the Antitrust Guidelines for the Licensing of Intellectual Property in 1995, regulating the antitrust enforcement policy of the US Department of Justice and the Federal Trade Commission with respect to the Licensing of Intellectual Property protected by patent, copyright, and trade secret law, and the protection of know-how.

626. The agencies are instructed to predict whether a practice is potentially anticompetitive. However, as section 1.0 lays down, the Guidelines cannot replace judgment and discretion in Antitrust Law enforcement. Moreover, the standards laid down in the Guidelines must be applied in unforeseeable circumstances. Each case will be evaluated in light of its own facts, and these Guidelines will be applied reasonably and flexibly. In the US, patents confer rights to exclude others from making, using, or selling in the US the invention claimed by the patent for a period of seventeen years from the date of issue of the patent.

627. It is recognized that the intellectual property laws and the Antitrust Laws share the common purpose of promoting innovation and enhancing consumer welfare.

628. The said section also states that the intellectual property laws provide incentives for innovation and its dissemination and commercialization by establishing enforceable property rights for the creators of new and useful products, more efficient processes, and original works of expression. In the absence of intellectual property rights, imitators could more rapidly exploit the efforts of innovators and investors, without any compensation for the latter. Rapid imitation would reduce the commercial value of innovation and erode incentives to invest, ultimately harming the consumers. The Antitrust Laws promote innovation and consumer welfare by prohibiting certain actions that may harm competition with respect to either existing or new ways of serving consumers.

629. Regarding market power, which is defined as the ability to profitably maintain prices above, or maintain output below, competitive levels for a significant period of time, the Guidelines state that the agencies should not presume that a patent, copyright, or trade secret necessarily confers market power on its owner. Although the intellectual property right confers the power to exclude with respect to the *specific* product, process, or work in question, there will often be sufficient actual or potential close substitutes for such product, process, or work to prevent the exercise of market power.

630. If a patent or other form of intellectual property does confer market power, that market power does not in itself offend the Antitrust Laws.

631. There are important similarities between the US Guidelines and the European Union's TTBE (Transfer of Technology Block Exemption). In both statutes, price fixing and market division among horizontal competitors are regulated among others.

632. The European approach is more detailed in comparison with the US Guidelines.

B. Trademark Licensing

633. There are no specific rules to discuss in connection with this matter under Uruguayan Antitrust Law.

C. Know-How and Trade Secret Licensing

634. There are no specific rules to discuss in connection with this matter under Uruguayan Antitrust Law.

Chapter 2. Dominant Undertakings' Prohibited Practices

635. Typically, the Antitrust Law prevailing in the world recognizes two types of illegal abuse of dominant position: exclusionary or exploitative. In cases of exclusionary abuse of dominant position, the anticompetitive behaviour punished by the law is the use of a dominant position to exclude competitors (whether real or potential). Whereas, in cases of exploitative abuse of dominant position, what is illegal is the imposition of prices and commercial conditions that are different from the ones that would exist if there had been effective competition in the market.

§1. Exploitative Practices

I. Excessive/Unfair Pricing

636. Excessive and unfair pricing could be considered anticompetitive conduct if fixed in a manner that involves abuse of a dominant position. Section 4, subsection A provides as a general rule, as already discussed, that such imposition of prices is considered illegal.

637. The fixing of excessive prices will typically be deemed an anticompetitive practice under the Uruguayan Law. Charging prices beyond what is reasonably expected or that have no connection with the market, due to the dominant position the company holds, will be considered an abuse and the conduct will be deemed illegal.

638. Whereas, in general, cases of unfair prices involve complaints from manufacturers and small- and medium-sized retailers regarding the prices set by large manufacturers or retailers.

639. The Uruguayan Antitrust Act purports to promote fair and free competition, and there is nothing in it against low prices. In fact, given that the Act's goal is the welfare of consumers, low prices will be beneficial from this perspective. There is nothing wrong with efficiency and profitability attracting customers. The problem is when inexpensive products affect the relevant market because prices were fixed in anticipation of an anticompetitive effect.

640. Unfair prices can be a large company's strategy wherein it sells a product at a low cost and compensates losses by profits made from the sale of other products, or by other sources the firm may have. Hence, the final objective of preventing unfair price-cutting is to maintain a fair, competitive market.

641. In Japan, for instance, according to the Japan Fair Trade Commission,[53] the fairness or unfairness of price-cutting is determined on the basis of three factors, as

53. Https://www.jftc.go.jp/en/policy_enforcement/fair_trade_practices.html.

follows: (a) the relationship of price to costs; (b) impact upon competitors; or (c) lack of a justifiable reason for the price cut.

642. In Uruguay, there is no such complete regulation. In principle, price-cutting is not banned unless it can be considered to constitute abuse, mainly, due to its goal of eliminating competition so as to increase prices in the future (known as predation).

643. In other countries, certain advertising practices such as announcing the sale of products at low prices when the company has no intention of selling the product at the said prices, are studied under this subject matter. However, in Uruguay, it can be a violation of Consumers' Act No. 17.250 but not a case of unfair prices.

644. Section 24 of the Uruguayan Consumers' Act laid down that the following would be considered as unlawful publicity: any information or communication stated in any advertisement or piece of publicity which is false, or that in any other way, even by omitting essential data, can mislead the consumer about the quantity, origin, or price of the products.

645. This kind of practice is definitely banned by Uruguayan Law, but the piece of legislation that contains provisions regarding them is the Consumers' Act and not the Uruguayan Antitrust Act.

II. Discrimination

646. An economic agent is deemed to have discriminated when for the same product or service it applies different conditions to individuals or companies, for example, in some commercial relations such as suppliers and distributors. This generally occurs in cases where agents are placed on different levels of the production process.

647. It can happen not only from the seller's point of view but also in situations wherein buyers have power over a specific relevant market whereby they can demand different and beneficial conditions. It can be the case of a big supermarket that demands beneficial conditions and if those are not granted, it excludes the supplier's products from its shelves.

648. Discrimination places a competitor in an inferior position in the market, due to the benefits his competitors will gain.

649. A seller is liable for price discrimination when it charges different prices to different buyers. Price discrimination is prohibited under section 4, subsection C of the Act, which provides that it is considered unlawful to unjustifiably apply to third parties different conditions for the same products. However, discrimination can also be found to have been made in terms of valid terms, delivery, credits, etc.

650. The above conduct is deemed illegal by Uruguayan Law and is expressly mentioned in the Act as being one of the prohibited practices. Nevertheless, to be deemed illegal the conduct is required to be unjustified and to purport to place the competitor in a disadvantageous position before the rest of his competitors.

651. A typical case of discrimination can be found wherein the discrimination is made in order to benefit a local branch of the supplier.

§2. Exclusionary Practices

652. Diego Galante[54] in the Uruguayan doctrine has defined 'exclusionary practices' as the conduct whose goal is to hinder new competitors' access to the market or to evict some of the competitors that act therein.

I. Predation

653. Predation is one of the most widely studied anticompetitive practices in the world and in Uruguay as well because, although antitrust legislation is quite recent in Uruguay, predatory practices have been on the radar of the agency from the very beginning of Uruguayan legislation.

654. Predation can be described as a commercial strategy of a big company made in order to eliminate competition, by selling a product at low cost, purporting to eliminate other competitors from the market and, ultimately, charge higher prices without any market control, so as to recover the loss incurred.

655. In the majority of cases, this is merely a strategy to eliminate competition from a relevant market, since prices cannot be maintained at a low level over a long period of time. As a result, the goal of the big company that applies this strategy is to eliminate competition, as a first step, by charging prices that cannot be matched by the competition which is thereby forced to leave the market. The big company, generally a multinational firm, can afford to sell its products at a loss for a period of time during which the rest of the competitors wither and eventually leave the market.

656. Large retailers, typically branches of multinational firms that receive support from headquarters can afford to set the prices really low, at levels which are inaccessible to competitors. As a result, if a consumer has the opportunity to buy the same product from a small retailer or a big retailer offering a 50% rebate, the consumer will not have trouble deciding where to buy. The problem herein is that after a year or so, the small retailers (typically locals) will have stopped selling and

54. Diego Galante, *Operaciones de adquisiciones y fusiones en la Nueva Legislación de Competencia*, CADE 21 Aug. 2007.

the big retailer, in the absence of competition will be free to multiply the prices and, as hence recover the losses previously incurred, thus adversely affecting customers.

657. In this scenario, not only is the market harmed by this kind of illegal practice but also the consumers, who after a beneficial period of time in which they received beneficial conditions in buying the products, are later forced to acquire the same products at a price that is higher and has no connection with the market price.

658. The Uruguayan doctrine agrees that a mere strategy of low prices does not prove the existence of predatory practices. If the multinational firm owing to its headquarters' support or pure efficiency is able to sell products at a low price and maintain the same over a period without applying the second part of the traditional predatory strategy (increasing prices after elimination of competition), this will not be considered anticompetitive in Uruguay.

659. Nevertheless, it is striking that the new Uruguayan Act did not expressly include this behaviour, since it is one of the most typical cases of anticompetitive conduct. This is even more noteworthy since the former Act No. 17.243, section 14, subsection E (equivalent to the new section 4 of the Act) expressly forbade predatory practices if practised in a systematic way and without justifiable commercial reasons.

660. However, it is the authors' opinion that a predatory practice will be deemed illegal if it coincides with one of the general principles laid down in section 2 of the Act, that is, if the predatory practice aims to limit, restrict, or hinder the competition it will be considered anticompetitive but not per se, and only if it cannot be reasonably justified.

661. Uruguay has learned from the American tradition in terms of predatory prices because, as said, a pricing strategy will not always be deemed a predatory practice.

662. In the US, the concept of 'predatory practices' has passed several stages before reaching its current position in US jurisprudence, which was crucial in the legal analysis made in Uruguay regarding predation.

663. As Gavil[55] has said:

> until recently, antitrust doctrine gave dominant firms murky guidance about how much they could increase output and how low they could set their prices in response to entry or expansion by a competitor. Antitrust Law provides two mechanisms for challenging predatory pricing: section 2 of the Sherman Act and section 2 (a) of the Robinson-Patman Act, which forbids certain forms of price discrimination. In the 1950s and 1960s, cases interpreting these provisions often accepted the idea that a dominant firm could use 'deep pockets' to

55. Gavil, *supra* n. 14, at 605.

finance below-cost sales and charge supracompetitive prices once the rival had departed. A number of decisions displayed solicitude for the smaller, vanquished target of a dominant firm's pricing strategy.

664. The authors cite, as being representative of the earlier view on predatory pricing in the US, the *Utah Pie* case[56] wherein the US Supreme Court upheld the position that the plaintiff had produced enough evidence to sustain a jury verdict of unlawful discrimination determining the anticompetitive practice in the fact that 'Continental' had charged prices 'less than its direct cost plus an allocation for overhead'.

665. Afterwards, as Gavil maintained, in the next two decades 'Courts generally accepted the idea that price-cost tests should anchor predatory pricing analysis. Most tribunals in this period treated pricing at or above average variable cost as creating a rebuttable presumption of legality.'

666. The leading case that made the American Supreme Court reformulate its predatory pricing test was the *Brooke Group* case[57] when the Court stated that no reasonable jury could have concluded that the defendant's (Brown & Williamson's) conduct was illegal. The last sentences of the ruling capture the essence of the new paradigm, as follows:

> We hold that the evidence cannot support a finding that Brown & Williamson's alleged scheme was likely to result in oligopolistic price coordination and sustained supracompetitive pricing in the generic segment of the national cigarette market. Without this, Brown & Williamson had no reasonable prospect of recouping its predatory losses and could not inflict the injury to competition the Antitrust Laws prohibit.

667. This decision was crucial in Uruguay because it was in line with this new paradigm that the doctrine built[58] the prerequisites of a predatory practice in Uruguay, as follows:

(a) Dominant Position of the predator firm in the market.
(b) Intention to eliminate competitors from the market.
(c) Creation of obstacles that prevent future competitors from entering the market, which makes it possible to keep the prices high.
(d) Finally making profits after the elimination of competitors.

56. *Utah Pie Co. v. Continental Baking co.*, 386 US. 685, 87 S. Ct. 1326 (1967).
57. *Brooke Group Ltd. v. Brown & Williamson Tobacco Corp*. US Supreme Court, 1993, 509 US. 209, 113 S. Ct. 2578, 125 L.Ed.2d. 168.
58. Martinez Blanco. *supra* n. 55, at 74.

668. Furthermore, Olivera Garcia[59] has maintained, that although in a short-term analysis predatory practices can be beneficial for consumers since they are able to acquire products at low prices, predation is a practice aimed towards obtaining an illegal overwhelming position in the market and distort the normal mechanisms of price fixing.

669. The Uruguayan Antitrust Agency, when the overruled act was in force, had the opportunity to adjudicate on a case of possible predation (the *Geant* case).[60] The case involved a multinational supermarket established in the suburbs of Montevideo in a place that had been showing a clear increase of population.

670. The supermarket opened its doors with a strategy of very low prices that eventually made many nearby, smaller stores close down. The agency analysed the case and concluded that the strategy was not illegal since the second stage of the predatory measure had not been executed. The supermarket had proved that it could maintain its low prices over a long period due to its efficiency and, when it did increase prices, the new prices were merely an adjustment of the former ones, and they were not compensating the money the supermarket had lost during the promotion period. In short, the lowered prices were stable and had emerged from the efficiency of the supermarket.

671. Predation will be deemed anticompetitive in the Uruguayan legal system, pursuant to section 2 of the Act, if the price fixing is unreasonable and aims to eliminate competition. However, it is possible to find cases in which practices that could seem predatory are not illegal, due to their reasonableness, for example, the selling of unfashionable clothes.

672. In this case, the goal of the measures adopted was not to eliminate competitors. In fact, the reason behind selling the clothes at reduced prices was to eliminate certain items that could not be sold at the same price as the new ones.

673. The case of loss leading is not considered a predatory strategy inasmuch as it does not meet the requirements referred to above. It is typically considered in Uruguay to be a legal advertising strategy.

674. The above is often referred to as an *advertising strategy* which permits sellers to attract consumers by lowering the prices of some products and gaining profits from other products that are overpriced or by increasing the prices of the same product in the future. In this way, below-cost pricing may enhance consumer welfare but implies a clear lack of information that can be considered unlawful.

675. The practice consists in pricing some 'leader' products at low costs so as to attract customers to the retailer, in order to make profits on other products sold by the company.

---

59. Olivera Garcia. *supra* n. 46, at 32.
60. Dnc-Mef, June 2004.

676. This practice is common in Uruguayan supermarkets. Companies offer a product at a lowered cost for a period of time purporting to make it agreeable to customers and, afterwards, increase the price and make the consumer buy it again in the future at a higher price. Also, a customer can be seduced by a product that is offered at a low cost wherein other products in the supermarket have higher prices. This is known as a 'price promotion' in Uruguay.[61]

677. In some cases, the said conduct is performed with the goal of gaining profits in the future while losing money in the present.

678. In Uruguay, loss leading, in itself, is not considered an anticompetitive practice but a legal marketing promotion. In some cases, these practices have been viewed in the light of cases of unfair competition among competitors and not as anticompetitive cases.

679. As Paula Algorta[62] has maintained, even when predatory practices are typically connected with the idea of eliminating competitors from the market, this practice may also be found in the context of other anticompetitive practices such as hindering the access of potential competitors to the market (section 4, subsection G of the Act).

680. Finally, although one of the most important and discussed issues in predatory pricing is the measure of cost to be considered for the test of predation, there is no reference in Uruguayan Law in connection with this problem.

More recently, the Uruguayan Agency has had the opportunity of ruling in two cases that involved predatory prices:

(1) *Case 12/2010. Resolution 12/2010 of September 11, 2012:* Former Uruguayan airline PLUNA reported before the Agency a competitor (BQB) that was, allegedly, performing predatory measures in the stretch Punta del Este-Porto Alegre. BQB refused responsibility, since it did not provide information regarding its tariffs, alleging confidentiality. However, the Agency considered that BQB incurred violation of the Act by not providing the corresponding documentation.
(2) *Case 21/2012. Resolution 64/2013 dated May 20, 2013*: In this case DW Service SRL (a bike rental company located in Punta del Este) brought an action against Banco ITAU and another company –Rulero Producciones S.R.L. – for an alleged violation of the Act. It was maintained that during the summer of 2013 Rulero Producciones and Banco ITAU concerted a commercial promotion whereby they provided the service of bike rental for free. The DW Services alleged that this was a 'predatory measure' since it was impossible to compete against a company that does not charge for its services. Moreover, that this measure was taken in order to eliminate competitors by abusing of a dominant position.

61. Martínez Blanco, *supra* n. 22, at 76.
62. Algorta, *supra* n. 54, at 55.

The Agency ruled in favour of the defendants by concluding that there was not a predatory measure in this case since to be predatory, the practice must purport to eliminate competitors and obtain benefits after applying the measure and this did not happen. Furthermore, it was considered as a promotional activity sponsored by Banco ITAU which was in favour of consumers and did not affect competition in an illegal way.

II. Tying

681. The Uruguayan Act also deals with this anticompetitive practice, in which certain contracts are forced by one agent, under an unlawful quid pro quo rationale.

682. Subsection D of section 4 lays down that it is a prohibited practice to make a deal subject to subsequent supplemental promises and obligations that due to their own nature or commercial uses, do not have any connection to the purpose of the contract.

683. Sellers that handle more than one product may seek to tie the sale of one (the one the customer wants) with another one (which is not asked for by the customer). In the US, such practices are governed by the general provisions of the Sherman Act, and in more detail by section 3 of the Clayton Act. The latter prohibits such arrangements if the more likely result is 'substantially to lessen competition'.

684. In the US, tying is per se unlawful if the seller possesses a sufficiently dominant position in the relevant market, and the buyer is obliged to buy the additional product as a precondition to buying the one he wants to buy.

685. It is the case, typically, in which one of the parties to a contract demands additional promises that have no connection with the main purpose of the contract.

686. An example of this prohibited practice is when a supplier asks the buyer to buy an additional product as a precondition in selling the product the buyer wants. Through this practice, the supplier seeks to take advantage of its main product so as to introduce into the market another product that is not well known in the market.

687. In general, these cases will be presented as an abuse of a dominant position by an economic agent.

688. In the US, some tying cases have been justified by exceptional competitive circumstances. For example, in new industries and as part of a franchise operation involving the licensing of the seller's trademark to franchisees.

689. The Uruguayan doctrine is consistent in not considering illegal the additional promises stated in a franchising agreement in which there are certain conditions that must be met by the franchisee to be able to qualify.

690. In the US, section 5.0 of the Antitrust Guidelines for the Licensing of Intellectual Property defines a 'tying' or 'tie-in' or 'tied sale' arrangement as 'an agreement by a party to sell one product (...) on the condition that the buyer also purchases a different (or tied) product, or at least agrees that he will not purchase that [tied] product from any other supplier'.[63]

III. Rebates

691. The issue of whether or not rebates can be considered anticompetitive practices has been mainly discussed in European law. Article 102 of the Treaty on the Functioning of the European Union tries to prevent practices of dominant firms that distort the normal functioning of the market.

692. In evaluating whether a discount or rebate scheme can qualify as an abuse under Article 102 TFEU, the European Courts have tried to determine whether the rebate scheme is objectively justified.

693. In Uruguay, there are no specific norms that consider rebate to be per se anti-competitive. However, if the rebate scheme is made in the context of an exclusionary or predatory practice, it would be illegal under Uruguayan Law.

694. For instance, if a supermarket applies a rebate scheme by lowering its prices in order to eliminate competition this will clearly be considered a predatory measure and consequently illegal. However, if rebates are granted as a promotion, commercially justified, for a period of time, it will typically be considered by Uruguayan Law to be a legal promotion.

695. There has not been any precedent in Uruguayan case law wherein decision makers adjudicated on a rebate case. The typical cases of rebates seen in the Uruguayan market are legal.

696. Under European Union Law, typically, all rebate policies by dominant firms that are not clearly related to quantities risk being deemed illegal. It cannot be stated that Uruguay has a similar principle. In a case involving rebate, the judge or the agency must determine whether or not the practice involves or in any other way affects competition and/or consumers.

IV. Refusal to Deal

697. In a vertical boycott agreement, as a general rule, a seller should not make an agreement with some of its customers that it will not sell to another. Section 4 provides for this situation and deems this practice illegal. As already pointed out,

63. *Eastman Kodak Co. v. Image Technical Services, Inc.*, 112 S. Ct. 2072, 2079 (1992).

the Act lays down that it is unlawful to prevent the access of competitors to infrastructures that are essential for the production, distribution, or commercialization of products, services, or productive infrastructure.

698. In the US, as Gavil[64] maintained:

> since the earliest days of the Sherman Act, section 2, monopolization cases have focused on alleged refusals by dominant firms to deal with their rivals, customers, or suppliers. Refusal to deal cases can be placed in three categories. The first category includes cases in which a dominant firm threatens to cease cooperation with a customer or supplier that is considering forming a relationship with the dominant firm's competitors. The second category consists of challenges to a dominant firm's attempt to withdraw from an existing contractual relationship or to impose new terms on an existing relationship. The third category concerns the refusal of a dominant firm to provide access to a facility – sometimes called an 'essential facility' – that a rival requires in order to compete with the dominant firm.

699. Under the Uruguayan Law, as previously explained,[65] this is one of the typical cases of restrictive agreements due to its way to avoid new competition.

700. However, as a general rule, a supplier has traditionally been allowed the right, to select those with whom it will do business. But if the said supplier concerts with other competitors not selling to a specific individual or company, it will constitute an anticompetitive practice.

A. Recent Case

701. Uruguay, due to the lack of regulation on this matter for a long time, does not have a great tradition in terms of antitrust legal actions. However, during the World Cup of 2010, an antitrust case was brought before the competent Authority in which the television channel Direct TV claimed the right to transmit the games (by paying the corresponding price), even though the three private television channels that owned the rights over the tournament refused to sell them to Direct TV. The attitude of the three channels, acting as a sort of cartel, was condemned by the Uruguayan Agency, which ordered them to sell the rights to Direct TV.

702. This case can be considered as a case of 'refusal to deal' in which the party that owned the rights refused to deal them to a local company. In fact, Direct TV said that it was worried about its subscribers who would be unable to access the games. Another important issue in this case was that there were three agents involved (three television channels) and only one refused to deal. Furthermore, it

64. Gavil, *supra* n. 14, at 630.
65. *See* p. 56 for more information.

was revealed that two of the three channels had an agreement with Direct TV to buy the rights for USD 450,000. However, one of the channels ruled out the possibility and, according to Direct TV, was never amenable to discuss a mutually agreeable price.

703. In this case, Direct TV's argument was that the television channel that refused to enter into a negotiation discriminated against one competitor which was in a non-dominant position.

V. Price Squeeze

704. As J. Gregory Sidak[66] has maintained, considering the American law, a price squeeze, or margin squeeze:

> is a theory of antitrust liability under section 2 of the Sherman Act that concerns a vertically integrated monopolist that sells its upstream bottleneck input to firms that compete with the monopolist's production of a downstream product sold to end users. At issue is the size of the margin between the monopolist's input price and its retail price. Recent antitrust price squeeze cases have split the U.S. Courts of Appeals. The D.C. Circuit has concluded that, because a vertically integrated monopolist may refuse to provide its upstream inputs to its downstream competitors, it may raise the price of its upstream inputs without incurring antitrust liability. On the other hand, the Ninth Circuit's 2007 linkLine decision rejected such reasoning, notwithstanding Trinko. Predicated on Judge Learned Hand's opinion in Alcoa, LinkLine subordinates the protection of consumers to the protection of competitors. It requires access-pricing analysis that more resembles the work of a public utilities commission than that of a federal judge in an antitrust case.

705. In Uruguay, price squeeze has been considered to be another abuse of dominant position and has been defined by Marcelo Amorín[67] in the Uruguayan doctrine as the practice in which a company needs a product that it produced to elaborate a more sophisticated one, that is, the company produces both products but one is the basis of the second. In this case, the company sells the remaining or excess of the first product, which it has not used, at a price that ensures that no other company can feasibly produce the second elaborated product. Using this scheme, the said company controls the price of the second product by manipulating the price of the first.

706. This practice is considered anticompetitive under Uruguayan Law, since it implies an abuse of the dominant position.

---

66. Gregory J. Sidak, *Abolishing the Price Squeeze as a Theory of Antitrust Liability*, 4 J. Competition L. & Econ. 279–309 (2008).
67. Amorin, *supra* n. 18, at 101.

707. It is unfortunate that there has not been any case dealing with this situation in Uruguayan case law.

Chapter 3. Concentrations

708. As has been discussed in the previous chapters, behaviours that jeopardize free competition can affect the efficiency of the market and ultimately affect the consumers, who are the ultimate beneficiaries of antitrust regulation in Uruguay. Whether the structures of a country's antitrust system are modified, this clearly can eliminate the necessary balance among the different agents of the market. If the control exercised by the various players in a certain relevant market is modified by eliminating the earlier independence and letting one player control the market, this will affect the market, in one way or another.

709. This corporate decision that can make that were used to be, effectively, more than one player there is now only one or two, making possible the existence of monopolies or oligopolies, can lead to concentration.

§1. The Uruguayan Regulation

710. As previously pointed out, section 7 of the Act lays down that the Uruguayan Antitrust Agency has to be notified of every act of economic concentration within certain thresholds set by law.

711. In the same section, it is said that potential acts of economic concentration are as follows:

> those operations which imply a modification in the control structure through: mergers of companies, acquisition of shares, membership interests or participations, acquisition of business as an ongoing concern, total or partial acquisition of corporate assets, and any other type of legally valid agreement which imply transferring the control of all or part of the economic units or enterprises.

§2. Horizontal Mergers

712. When a company buys some or all of the stock or assets of another, the transaction will be considered as an acquisition. However, if all of a company is acquired, the two entities will merge one into each other. The latter case involves one of the two types of mergers which Law No. 16060 regulates, which imply at the end of the deal that one of them is absorbed by the other, erasing, as a consequence, the first one. The other type of merger regulated by Uruguayan Law is the one wherein two or more companies form a new company by erasing the ones that created it.

713. As Gavil[68] has stated:

> mergers and acquisitions among horizontal rivals can reduce competition because they alter the structure of markets by changing the number, identity, size and other characteristics of firms. (…) Mergers and acquisitions commonly are categorized as 'horizontal', 'vertical' and 'conglomerate'. Like horizontal agreements, horizontal mergers and acquisitions involve sellers of substitutes, i.e., competitors; like vertical mergers and acquisitions involve firms and their suppliers, customers, or other sellers of complements; and conglomerate mergers involve firms that sell neither substitutes nor complements. Typically, a conglomerate is engaged in many unrelated lines of business.

714. In the US, the main provision regarding horizontal mergers is section 7 of the Clayton Act, according to which, stock or asset deals among corporations whose ultimate effect is to affect competition or create monopolies are prohibited.

715. As Gavil has said, the distinguishing characteristic of the anti-merger prohibitions of the Clayton Act is its objection to mergers that 'may substantially lessen competition'.

716. As in other cases, one of the most important issues to resolve is whether or not the relevant market was affected, and to first determine the extent of the relevant market.

717. In Uruguay, the analysis of whether or not a certain merger can be deemed to be an illegal concentration should be analysed in the light of the two thresholds laid down by Uruguayan Law.

718. In analysing the new participation of the conglomerated company in the relevant market, it will be necessary to consider the proportion of this new company in the context of the market in comparison with the rest of the players of the market, the tendency that this concentration shows in the Uruguayan market, among other factors.

I. Recent Cases of Horizontal Mergers in the Banking Sector

719. In May 2010, the Spanish bank BBVA, through its Uruguayan subsidiary Banco Bilbao Vizcaya Argentaria Uruguay S.A., executed an agreement with the French bank Credit Agricole S.A., for the purchase of the Uruguayan banking operations of Credit Agricole. The purchase included Credit Uruguay Banco S.A. (full licence Bank), Emprendimientos de Valor S.A. (consumer credit Company), and Credit Agricole Distribuidora de Seguros S.R.L (insurance broker).

68. Gavil, *supra* n. 14, at 418.

720. The closing of the deal occurred in May 2011, since authorizations from the Uruguayan and Spanish banking regulators were necessary. Once the acquisition was completed, BBVA Uruguay became Uruguay's third largest banking institution, with 12% of the market share, after Republic Bank (owned by the state) and Banco Santander.

721. Another noteworthy case occurred by the end of 2008 when Banco Santander, in an asset deal, acquired ABN Amro's Montevideo branch, creating the largest private bank in Uruguay.

722. After the merger's approval by Uruguay's Executive and the Central Bank, the resulting bank obtained a 20% share of Uruguay's private banking market.[69]

§3. Vertical Mergers

723. As in the US, vertical mergers in Uruguay are subject to the same rules as horizontal mergers. However, as in the US, certain principles applicable to horizontal mergers can vary when dealing with vertical mergers.

724. When the merger is vertical, one competitor of a relevant market merges into another company that is below or above it in the production chain, and the effects of the merger can lead to a dominant position of the surviving company, which can eventually possess the power of price fixing with the effects already discussed.

725. However, it is also possible to see anticompetitive effects of a vertical merger towards suppliers. If two or more distributors of a specific product in a certain market merge, the surviving entity will have a substantial amount of power when negotiating with suppliers, which can bring about anticompetitive effects.

§4. Market/Product Extension Mergers

726. The concept is not applicable to the Uruguayan system.

§5. Pure Conglomerate Mergers

727. When companies that are not connected with each other vertically or horizontally enter into an agreement, it is called a conglomerate merger. For example, when a company in the forestry sector merges with another one which is in a different sector such as the pharmaceutical sector. The result of this merger is a conglomerate of companies that act in many different sectors which are not competing with each other.

---

69. El Economista Newspaper, Madrid 3 May 2010.

728. These kind of companies are well known in the US, but due to the limited size of the Uruguayan market, is not part of the latter.

729. As Prof. Cabanellas de las Cuevas[70] has maintained, there is an array of reasons that made the formation of this conglomerates important across the world, which are, among others, the following: the use of surplus, best risk management, best access to the markets, and financing costs.

§6. Joint Ventures

730. The International doctrine has categorized joint ventures into three types, as follows:

(a) Research and Development.
(b) Production.
(c) Distribution.

731. Following Gavil's[71] analysis, the Research and Development joint ventures are the best known because using this structure, the intellectual and financial resources of firms – often rivals – are combined to pursue the development of a new product, for instance, joint forces. Production joint ventures are formed to produce something; typically a new product and Distribution joint ventures combine the capabilities of firms to bring new or existing products or services to the market. They can combine, improve, or expand existing capabilities that can lead to the creation of new capabilities or methods.

732. The formation of joint ventures can lead to collusive and exclusionary practices not only in the US but also in Uruguay. As Gavil says, 'by combining the research or productive capabilities of competing firms that collectively possess market power, a joint venture substitutes joint for individual action cooperation for competition. It can serve, therefore, as just another vehicle for setting prices, reducing innovation or restricting some other dimension of competition'.

733. Under Uruguayan Law, a joint venture agreement, in any of its types, will be considered as another economic concentration. In such cases, apart from mergers, we will be dealing with an external concentration since it will arise out of an agreement, as in the studied case of franchising, and not, typically, out of a corporate transaction.

734. There is no specific test in Uruguay to distinguish between a cooperative joint venture and a concentrative joint venture.

70. Cabanellas De Las Cuevas, *supra* n. 31, at 631.
71. Gavil, *supra* n. 14, at 203.

735. The concentration derived from a joint venture agreement should be viewed under the same thresholds as already discussed when analysing mergers and acquisition. For instance, if two companies together enter into an agreement and both together reach or exceed 50% of the relevant market, the obligation to notify the agency of the concentration will arise in the same terms as in the case of any other economic concentration.

Part III. Administrative Procedure

Chapter 1. Administrative Investigations before the Antitrust Authority

§1. INITIATIVE

I. General Sectors Inquiries

736. In the European system, the Authority has the power to conduct general inquiries on single economic sectors. These inquiries are not aimed at ascertaining any specific illegal conduct, but rather at assessing the general competitive dynamics of a particular sector or industry.

737. Uruguayan Law does not provide for such power.

II. Ex Officio Investigations

738. Investigations can be commenced, extended, or followed ex officio.

739. First, the Commission does not require any reporting party to start an investigation. This is harmonious with the spirit of Antitrust Law which refers to the protection of the market and the consumers.

740. The fact is that it would not always be easy to identify a person interested enough to report the conduct that ought to be investigated. However, the facts are relevant per se if they indicate that there is a substantial possibility that anticompetitive practices may be taking place, regardless of whether or not there is a reporting party. In addition, some of these practices affect mainly the consumers who, presumably, are not organized enough to report the said conduct.

741. To enable the necessary investigations, the Commission has the faculty to request information from companies, associations, chambers of commerce, industries, or any other entities which may be able to provide relevant information.

742. In this regard, it should be noted that issues such as the determination of the relevant market, usually determine the necessity of these inquiries.

743. Also, the Commission may extend the investigations to other individuals ex officio when, in addition to the individuals or entities indicated in a report as being presumably responsible for the conduct investigated, the Commission identifies others that could be also liable.

744. Finally, according to section 22 of Decree 404/07, an investigation initiated pursuant to a report submitted by an individual, can be followed ex officio when the reporting party desists.

III. Complaints

745. According to section 21 of Decree 404/07, any individual or entity, public or private, national or foreign, is entitled to report to the Commission the occurrence of prohibited practices.

746. To report a forbidden practice, the interested party should submit a writ containing certain minimum information: identification of the person filing the report, precise description of the conduct presumably anticompetitive, as well as all and any means of evidence to support the description.

747. In cases with sufficient grounds, the reporting individual or entity may request that its name not be disclosed.

748. When an allegedly anticompetitive conduct is reported, the Commission grants a ten-working-day term to analyse the writ and evidence submitted and decide if the investigation should be initiated or not. In case it is decided that the investigation shall be initiated, the same is notified to the individuals presumably responsible for the conduct reported.

749. Section 22 of Decree 404/07 states that the individual who has reported a presumably anticompetitive practice, may desist from it and communicate the same to the Commission. In such a case, the Commission is entitled to decide whether the investigation is to be followed ex officio or closed.

750. In the course of the investigations, many decisions are required to be made, which can potentially affect the parties involved or third parties. For example, the requirement of information from a third party who considers it excessive or very expensive to be produced or considers it to be within professional secrecy; a piece of evidence which is rejected on the ground of it being irrelevant; the decision of requesting judicial measures, etc.

751. All these decisions are formally administrative acts and consequently can be challenged by means of administrative appeals which ordinarily do not suspend the proceedings.

§2. POWERS

I. Request for Information

752. The powers of the Commission to require information are broad. This information may be related to several aspects relevant to the conduct of an investigation, to determine a relevant market, or to otherwise facilitate the Commission perform its various duties.

753. The Act also lays down the consequent obligation of collaborating for every person (individual or legal entity, national or foreign, public or private), who will be compelled to provide the Commission with '*all information within their knowledge and all documents in their power*' within the term of ten days counted from the day following the day in which the request was made.

754. This is a very sensitive matter, and fortunately the Act rightly establishes that the obligations of collaborating do not imply the obligation to reveal *commercial secrets, maps, 'know how', inventions, formulas, patents.* In the authors' opinion, although not stated as exceptions, other confidential duties such as those deriving from professional and privileged bank-related information, must be understood to constitute reasonable grounds to excuse compliance with a requirement to provide information.

755. In the event of non-compliance with the obligation of collaborating with the Commission, sanctions identical to those that could be imposed in the event of violation of antitrust rules can be imposed on the person not complying.

II. Investigating and Search Powers

756. In addition to requesting information, the Commission is entitled to request from the Courts the adoption of reserved measures to gather evidence, such as the exhibition and obtaining of copies of civil or commercial documents, company's books, company ledger, and accounting databases. These measures may be adopted without giving the affected parties any prior notice.

757. Some of these measures are really useful in the investigating process. In this sense, the 'prohibition to innovate' is intended to prevent the alteration of the factual or legal situation. This is the kind of measure that ensures relevant pieces of evidence. In addition, the 'preventive attachment or seizure' of documents can assure that relevant documents are not destroyed or erased, thus enabling the Commission to secure relevant evidence.

758. Not only the individuals and entities involved in the investigation but also any person with relevant information is under the obligation to render the information in his possession (section 14 of the Act). As a result, if this obligation is not complied with, the Commission can consider it a violation of the Act (due to the obstruction it causes to the investigation) and sanction the wrongdoer.

759. Whereas, section 24 of Decree 404/2007 set forth that the Commission can, due to the special circumstances of the case, declare that the case should be conducted in a confidential manner. Moreover, in accordance with section 29 of the same decree, business confidentiality is granted, which means that business secrets, patents, know-how, etc. are not expected to be released in any case.

III. Cooperation with Other State Institutions

760. Section 16 of Decree 404/07 expressly refers to the relations that the Commission should have with other state institutions.

761. In this regard, the Commission should issue recommendations to the Executive and Legislative Powers regarding promotion of competition and/or any legal amendments that the Commission may deem necessary.

762. In addition, the Commission should assist the URSEA, the URSEC, and the Central Bank when required by said entities, to help in the application of Antitrust Laws.

763. Last but not least, section 16 of Decree 404/07 set out that the Commission is entitled to establish relations with other organs in charge of the application of Antitrust Laws, whether in Uruguay or abroad and to participate in all and any forum in which antitrust issues may be discussed or negotiated; in this last instance, in coordination with other governmental entities.

IV. A MERCOSUR Trade Committee

764. Uruguay is a member of the South American Economic Organization (*Mercado Comúndel Sur*-MERCOSUR) which is a regional integration process that has among its objectives to encourage a common space that generates commercial opportunities and investments through the competitive integration of each Member States' national economies.

The MERCOSUR Trade Committee is allowed, for the instrumentation of common trade policies, to create technical committees, one of them (No. 5) is called Defence of Competition. This committee is responsible for the compliance of the general guidelines provided for Dec. CMC Nº21/94, regarding prohibited antitrust behaviours and cooperation between the Member States to identify and punish antitrust conducts.

Act No. 19.173 from January 2014 approves the MERCOSUR Agreement for the Defense of Competition held in Brazil in 2010 (hereinafter the 'Agreement'). The Agreement intends to promote cooperation and coordination between Member States in the application of competition regulation inside MERCOSUR. It also establishes the way in which each member can make consults related to the content of the Agreement to Committee No. 5. Furthermore, it provides with guidelines to perform coordination activities in order to resolve cases in similar ways and to exchange information and experiences on the matter.

§3. Right of Defence

I. Content and Notification of Opening Decisions

765. According to the procedure referred to in sections 18–38 of Decree 404/07, the opening decision may be adopted either ex parte or ex officio.

766. The opening decision is issued when the Commission deems that anticompetitive conducts may be taking place in a relevant market, and it is hence necessary to determine the facts and eventual liabilities.

767. This Act is notified to the interested party inasmuch as the Commission is aware of the address, otherwise it is published.

768. The individual and/or entity notified that an investigation has been initiated by the Commission, is granted a ten-working-day term, to be counted from the day following the service, to produce a response in relation to the facts mentioned by the reporting party.

769. When filing the response, all and any evidence deemed necessary should be submitted or clearly indicated if it is to be collected.

II. The Proceedings: Hearings, Access to File, Briefs

770. In all matters not expressly addressed by Decree 404/07, the proceedings must be conducted in accordance to Decree 500/91 which deals with administrative proceedings in general.

771. Access to files is free unless the Commission states the contrary on the grounds that confidential information is contained within the file. The right to access the file comprehends the right to obtain a copy of it. The access is free not only to the parties of a specific case but also to third parties.

772. Decisions are taken without any requirement of the parties being requested to attend a hearing.

773. Hearings may take place when depositions are needed and to request further clarifications of the respective positions of the parties.

774. The Act enables the Commission to suspend the administrative proceedings for two purposes: (1) the purpose of arriving, with the alleged offender, to the decision to cease or modify the conduct under investigation or (2) the purpose of considering a possible settlement agreement between the reported party and the person who reported the conduct, when it is a case of abuse of dominant position and the only person suffering the consequences is the one who reported the conduct.

775. The authors believe that in this last case the solution is not correct. Antitrust Law must be focused, in principle, on the market, defending a wide interest and not the economic agent's concrete or individual interests.

776. In principle, parties are not allowed to submit further documents to the proceeding, different from the ones specifically required by the law.

III. Statement of Objections

777. In the law of the European Union, there is a stage in which the Antitrust Authority sends to the parties a full statement of objections upon the investigation's conclusion.

778. Uruguayan Law does not provide for any such statement of objections.

IV. Final Hearing and Decision

779. Final decision cannot be validly taken unless the investigated party has had enough opportunity to exercise its right of defence, which includes the right to submit all and any evidence available, except for those that can be legally rejected by the Commission.

780. Uruguayan Law does not establish a final hearing of the parties before the Authority takes the final decision. Once the various steps specifically set forth by law are complied with, the Authority can take the decision.

781. The final decision can be appealed if considered illegitimate.

A. Participation of Third Parties

782. As expressed above, all and any aspects of the procedure not defined by Decree 404/07 should be decided in accordance with Decree 500/91.

783. Section 17 of Decree 500/91 states that all third parties which may be affected by the decisions to be taken in an administrative file have the right to appear before the authorities, request a copy of the file, and submit writs and evidence.

784. As a result, pursuant to this rule any affected party is entitled to protect its interests and therefore have the right to access the file.

Chapter 2. Voluntary Notifications and Clearance Decisions

785. There are no specific rules to discuss in connection with this matter under Uruguayan Antitrust Law.

Chapter 3. Merger Control

§1. Preliminary Filing Obligations

I. Criteria and Thresholds

786. One of the biggest innovations of the Act was the creation of a government control mechanism in economic concentration transactions, which intends to prevent economic concentrations that can lead to antitrust behaviours. This kind of control had been in existence in the US since the Sherman Act of 1890, in various countries of Latin America, as well as, recently, in Europe. However, given both the lack of antitrust regulation Uruguay has had for most of its history and the existing international patterns, some kind of government control in M&A transactions was deemed necessary and was ultimately created in 2007.

A. Criteria

787. Regarding concentrations, the Uruguayan Congress largely discussed which of the two models regarding M&A authorizations/notifications, applied across the world (*ex ante* and *ex post*), was more suited to the Uruguayan characteristics. There were supporters of both sides and none could refute the other's stand. In light of this dichotomy, the solution was that the control should be made neither *ex ante* nor *ex post.* A hybrid solution emerged from the discussion of the bill since it is neither a typical pre-merger authorization nor an ex post facto resolution. The Uruguayan Act called for a 'notification' that is required to be made in certain specific cases, as will be discussed.

B. Thresholds

788. According to the Act, there is an obligation to notify the corresponding Uruguayan Agency of acts of economic concentration, such as mergers and acquisitions, *ten days before* such acts are executed by companies, provided that such acts fulfil *any* of the following requirements:

(1) When as a consequence of the transaction, the market share of the combined entity becomes equal to or above 50% of the relevant market.
(2) When the gross annual invoice in the Uruguayan territory of the participants in the transaction is equal to or above USD 75,000,000 in any of the last three financial years.

789. The American system, as the Uruguayan one, has a threshold notification proceeding. According to section 801.1 of the Hart-Scott-Rodino Antitrust Improvements Act of 1976, the term 'notification threshold' means the following:

(1) A total amount of voting securities and assets of the acquired person valued at greater than UYU 50 million but less than UYU 100 million.
(2) A total amount of voting securities and assets of the acquired person valued at UYU 100 million or greater but less than UYU 500 million.
(3) A total amount of voting securities and assets of the acquired person valued at UYU 500 million or greater.
(4) Twenty-five per cent of the outstanding voting securities of an issuer if valued at greater than UYU 1 billion; or
(5) Fifty per cent of the outstanding voting securities of an issuer if valued at greater than UYU 50 million.

790. As for some Uruguayan neighbours, both Brazil and Argentina followed the US system. Argentina struck down Act No. 22.262 and passed Act No. 25.156 which not only tried to prevent abuse of dominant position but also tried to control economic concentration when it could affect competition, by requiring pre-merger authorizations. Brazil has also followed the US system earlier (Act No. 4137/62 and Act No. 8884/1994) requiring pre-merger authorizations.[72]

791. Notwithstanding this, section 8 provides four exceptions in which there is no obligation to notify, even when some of the above-mentioned conditions occur. They are the following: (a) the acquisition of companies in which the buyer already had at least 50% of its shares; (b) the acquisition of bonds, debentures, obligations, any other security issued by the company, or shares with no voting rights; (c) the acquisition of only one company by only one foreign company which previously did not possess assets or shares of other companies in the country; (d) acquisitions of companies, which have or have not declared bankruptcy, which have not registered any activity within the country in the previous year.

792. Section 16 of the Decree 404/007 set forth in subsection H that among the legal authorities of the agency was *included* the Authority to issue special rulings and answer questions regarding whether a prospective merger or an acquisition that has been prepared can be considered to be an economic concentration operation.

793. In this case, the opinion of the agency will be bound, which can make convenient asking the agency if the company that will be the result of the economic concentration can be considered to be within the thresholds mentioned above.

794. It is clear that the prior question that interested parties can ask the agency to confirm if they must notify regarding the merger or acquisition is not mandatory, but it is certainly convenient. The merging companies announcing the project to the government at a prior stage could be inconvenient.

---

72. Berdaguer, *supra* n. 12, at 126.

II. Turnover Calculation

795. As already pointed out, one of the situations that triggers the obligation to notify the agency is when the gross annual invoice in Uruguayan territory of the participants in the transaction is equal to or above USD 75,000,000 in any of the last three financial years.

796. Uruguayan Law does not set forth any further criteria for calculation.

III. Market Share Calculation

797. The other situation that makes the notification necessary is when, as a consequence of the transaction, the economic concentration equals or exceeds 50% of the relevant market.

798. The agency shall consider, in order to determine the market share, only the relevant market, in line with the concept discussed above.

IV. Other Relevant Notions

A. Monopolies in Fact

799. If a merger produces the formation of a monopoly in fact, in the terms of section 9 of the Act, a mere notification will not be enough and the government must authorize the transaction.

800. In this special case of economic concentration, considering the risks related to anticompetitive effects, a mere notification is not enough and a government authorization is required.

801. The details of this authorization have already been discussed in the Chapter titled 'Concentrations'.

802. Section 9 of the Act, subsection 1 set forth that in cases wherein the economic concentration implies the formation of a monopoly in fact, the said process must '*be authorized*' by the agency.

803. It is clear that the case of formation of monopolies in fact is different from the perspective of Uruguayan Law, from the other cases of economic concentrations when one of the thresholds is reached. As a result, when a monopoly in fact has been created, the agency must authorize it.

804. Pursuant to section 42, subsection 2 of the Decree 404/007 a monopoly in fact is said to be formed when after the concentration process only one company emerges in the relevant market, defined by the agency in the same year when the concentration happened or in any of the two previous years counting from the submission of the Authorization Request. Provided there is a difference between the analysis made by the interested parties and the agency, the one prepared by the latter will prevail.

805. According to section 9 of the Act, the existence of the relevant market is one of the factors that should be taken into consideration, but it is also necessary to consider external competition and the efficiency that can be achieved with the monopoly in fact.

806. The Act does not stipulate exactly when the interested party should submit the Authorization Request. However, Decree 404/007 laid down that it has to be made 'previously', and the effective monopolistic concentration cannot be performed until authorization is granted by the agency.

807. Notwithstanding the foregoing, section 42, subsection 2 of the Decree 404/2007 lays down that the interested parties can provisorily register the concentration instrument (e.g., the merger agreement) with the Uruguayan Trade Registry. The parties must also declare that the governmental authorization had not yet been granted.

808. This 'provisory register' seems to be inconsistent with the general principle that the authorization must be prior to the economic concentration.

809. Furthermore, as it was explained, 'monopolies in fact' are only prohibited in certain cases. When there is no alternative way, for instance, to supply a certain product to a small town which can only have one producer or distributor, the monopoly will be tolerated by the system due to the benefit it provides to consumers. The group that is intended to be protected by law and the final beneficiaries of the antitrust system in Uruguay are supposed to be the consumers. If in a particular case, to defend consumers' rights it is necessary to consider as legal a certain situation that in most instances would be against the law, the protection of the consumers' rights will prevail.

810. As previously explained – and as will be examined in the last chapter of this book – Uruguayan Law does not require a pre-merger authorization, though in cases of 'monopolies in fact' a specific authorization is required.

B. Analysis and Evaluation

811. The agency must evaluate on a case-by-case basis whether or not a monopoly in fact has been formed and if the latter should be authorized. In order to find out if the monopoly in fact could be considered beneficial for the system, three factors should be taken into account, as follows:

(a) *Relevant Market*: The relevant market affected by the economic concentration.

(b) *External Competition*: The Uruguayan firms are small as compared to multinational firms, which is a disadvantage if it wants to compete internationally. For this reason, the external competition has to be considered by the Agency when authorizing the monopoly.
(c) *Efficiency*: Whether the benefit for consumers can only be achieved through a monopoly in fact, since there is not enough of a market for more than one competitor. Anticompetitive measures cannot go so far as to artificially create competitors when this is not possible in a given market.

812. As previously stated, in Uruguay, the beer sector is a monopoly in fact, which is authorized by the government. After corporate transactions that involved the Uruguayan beer companies, the effective control of all of them was placed in only one multinational company (namely AmBev Company).

813. This situation has been presented in the Uruguayan market for several years authorized by the government. It is clear that the latter is always overzealously controlling the acts of the monopoly in fact since, considering its dominant position in the market, it is more likely to carry out an anticompetitive conduct.

C. *Automatic Authorization*

814. Pursuant to section 9 of the Act, if the agency cannot issue a resolution in ninety days since the making of the Authorization Request, authorization will be considered to have been automatically granted.

§2. Structure of Proceedings

I. Preliminary Assessment and Full Investigation

815. The Uruguayan Congress largely discussed which of the two models regarding economic concentration authorizations/notifications applied across the world (*ex ante* or *ex post*) was more suited to the Uruguayan characteristics. There were supporters of both sides and none could overcome the other's position. In light of this dichotomy, the solution was that the control should be made neither *ex ante* nor *ex post*. A hybrid solution emerged from the discussion of the bill, since it is neither a typical pre-merger authorization nor an ex post facto resolution. The Uruguayan Act called for a 'Notification' that must be made in certain specific cases.

816. Uruguay approved a particular *ex ante* notification which is neither a pre-M&A authorization nor an *ex post* proceeding that cannot jeopardize the economic concentration transaction, in itself, since no authorization is expected after the notification. Although it is an *ex ante* notification, the control that can eventually occur will involve an analysis of the effects (*ex post*) of the concentration (which is not deemed illegal in itself).

817. A pure *ex ante* mechanism has been viewed by some lawmakers as inconvenient for a small country such as Uruguay. An *ex ante* mechanism would operate against the Uruguay's opportunities to gain foreign investments, since the necessity of a pre-M&A authorization, which can be time-consuming, would discourage investors.

818. However, it was deemed by the majority of the Uruguayan lawmakers that the efficiency of an *ex post* notification would be very less, because by the time the notification is made, the entire transaction is completed.[73]

819. Challenging the transaction after consummation creates uncertainty for the merged entity and its employees for a substantial period of time, whereas reviewing it with the benefit of hindsight, in theory, permits Courts to judge mergers on the basis of their actual effects.[74]

820. Furthermore, Prof. Cabanellas de las Cuevas[75] stated that an *ex post* mechanism can generate huge costs uncertainty, and it is generally not possible to remedy the antitrust effects of the concentration once performed.

821. In light of the above, the Uruguayan Act introduced a solution which is hybrid and two-pronged:

(a) It is not a typical pre-merger authorization, because the economic concentration does not depend on the government authorization.
(b) It is not an *ex post* authorization, because the notification does not request an authorization that can affect the merger or the acquisition.

II. Time Framework

822. According to the Act, there is an obligation to notify the agency of acts of economic concentration, such as mergers and acquisitions, *ten days before* such acts are executed by companies, provided that such acts fulfil either of the two thresholds extensively discussed in this book.

823. The Act created an *ex ante notification*, which must be made ten days before the transaction, but the government does not intend to approve it before closing. The idea of the notification is to make the government aware of the concentration so that it can observe whether due to the merger or the acquisition, antitrust practices are performed. In this case, the situation will be viewed under the same rules as any other case regulated by Uruguayan Law. The notification was referred to by one lawmaker as a 'yellow light'.

73. Martinez Blanco, *Manual … supra* n. 55, at 220.
74. Gavil, *supra* n. 14.
75. Cabanellas De Las Cuevas, *supra* n. 31.

824. If the companies which are part of an M&A transaction that triggers section 7 do not notify the agency within the ten-day period granted by law, the transaction will not be void or voidable. It will be completely enforceable.[76]

825. However, the agency can impose administrative sanctions on the companies that have not, in a timely manner, complied with the obligation to notify.

826. Finally, in order to avoid the said sanctions, the Uruguayan Act (section 19 of the Decree 404/2007) allows the filing of a preliminary proceeding whereby the companies planning an M&A, which can be covered by section 7, can ask the agency whether or not they need to provide the notification.

III. Right of Defence

827. Since there is no proceeding here that can potentially jeopardize the deal, and the involved parties are required only to notify the existence of an M&A transaction that can eventually affect competition, the parties do not need to exercise any right of defence at this point.

§3. Clearance and Conditional Clearance

I. Conditions and Undertakings

A. Content

828. There is no relevant issue to discuss in connection to this point under Uruguayan Law.

B. Timing

829. There is no relevant issue to discuss in connection to this point under Uruguayan Law.

§4. Relations with Other Merger Control Authorities

I. Other Authorities within the Local Jurisdiction

830. In accordance with section 27 of the Act, competition cases involving banks should be examined by the Uruguayan Central Bank and are not reviewed by the agency.

76. Berdaguer, *supra* n. 12, at 127.

831. In fact, when two or more banks are facing a merger, they have to operate as any other company whether or not any of the two thresholds has been reached. The Uruguayan Central Bank will decide the case within the same framework as any other case because the only legal modification is in terms of the enforcement agency.

832. In such cases, wherein banks are involved, the Uruguayan Antitrust Authority does not play any role in the enforcement process.

833. Furthermore, under Uruguayan Law, the Executive Power, through the Ministry of Finance, has to authorize a merger between banks before the agreement is executed. This administrative proceeding is a complement to the one brought before the Uruguayan Central Bank. There is no specific rule providing that the said Ministry can raise issues regarding possible anticompetitive behaviour, as part of its opinion. The Uruguayan Central Bank is the only Authority that can analyse this matter.

II. International Coordination

834. Uruguayan Law does not set forth any general principle in terms of international coordination. However, this does not imply that the Uruguayan system, as a whole, does not promote international coordination in antitrust issues.

835. However, as already discussed in this book, the law lays down in section 3 that this piece of legislation is also applicable to foreign individuals and firms that affect Uruguayan market. It is evident that in order to enforce this section, Uruguay will need the cooperation of international jurisdictions.

Chapter 4. Challenging of the Administrative Decision

§1. Competent Courts

836. According to the Uruguayan legal system, any decision of the Commission is an 'administrative act', as it is an expression of the administration's will aimed to produce legal effects. Administration here refers to any governmental entity acting within its administrative powers.

837. Within the category of administrative acts, the one issued by the Commission at the end of an investigation must be considered a Resolution (hereinafter the 'Resolution'), as it is a particular and concrete decision contained by the administrative act. (section 120 of Decree 500/91).

838. Since the Resolution is an administrative act, it can be challenged by the means established in section 317 of the Uruguayan Constitution and concordant laws. This section – in the part relevant herein – establishes the following:

> Administrative acts may be challenged by means of the revocation appeal to be filed before the same Authority which has issued them within the term of ten days to be counted from the first day after the personal notification of the act, if such notification should correspond, or from its publication in the Official Gazette.
> When the administrative act is issued by an entity which is subject to hierarchy, it may also be challenged by means of the hierarchic appeal, which must be filed at the same time as the revocation appeal and in subsidy of such appeal.

839. Therefore, the Resolution that entails an administrative act issued by the Commission, which is an entity subject to hierarchy, may have been challenged by the filing of both the revocation appeal and the subsidiary hierarchic appeal. In specific terms, the appeals should be addressed as follows: the revocation appeal to the Commission and the hierarchic appeal to the Executive Power as defined in section 149 of the Uruguayan Constitution, that is, as the head of the Executive Branch, also termed Executive Power.

840. The revocation and hierarchic appeals may be based on legal grounds as well as on matters relating to the opportunity or merit.

841. When administrative appeals fail and the administration does not revoke the Resolution, an annulment of the Resolution can be pursued before the competent Court, namely the *Contentious Administrative Court.*

842. According to the Uruguayan Constitution, the only entity which has the jurisdiction necessary to resolve the annulment of an administrative act in a contentious venue is the Contentious Administrative Court (sections 307 and subsequent sections in the Constitution), which is absolutely independent of the Judicial

Power. This Court cannot amend such acts and must limit itself to either annulling or confirming the acts it must adjudicate upon (section 311 of the Constitution).

843. To obtain the annulment of an administrative act by this Court, it is necessary to do the following: (i) provide evidence that the administrative act is contrary to a rule of law, understanding that 'rule of law' means all the basic principles of law or constitutional, legislative, regulatory, or contractual rules (Clause a) of section 23 of Act No. 15.524 – Contentious Administrative Court Act; or that when it was issued there was a deviation (section 309 of the Constitution), abuse, or excess of power (Clause a) of section 23 of Act No. 15.524 – Supreme Administrative Court Act and (ii) complete the administrative venue by means of the filing of the corresponding appeals (section 319 of the Constitution).

844. Not having filed the revocation and hierarchic administrative appeals in due time and manner impedes the fulfilment of the requisite of completing the administrative venue, and therefore hinders every chance of having the Contentious Administrative Court consider the annulment of the Resolution.

845. If an interested party wants to obtain a compensation for damages caused by a public entity, the situation is different. First, it should be determined what has caused the damage, if it is only a conduct or a decision made by the Authority.

846. If it is only a conduct, the affected party may claim damages directly before an Administrative Contentious Court, which is part of the structure of the Judicial Power.

847. If there is a decision made by the Antitrust Authority, actually infringing the antitrust rules and causing the damage, then the affected party may have the option of either of the following: (i) to claim directly the damages or (ii) to try to obtain the resolution is declared null and void by the administrative tribunal – which is independent of the Judicial and Executive Power – and then claim the damages. In this last course of action, if the resolution is not declared null and void or the action to claim damages is not 'reserved', the claim for damages cannot be brought.

§2. Time Limits

848. In order to have validly challenged the Resolution, the revocation appeal and the subsidiary hierarchic appeal must have been filed within the uninterrupted term of ten days to be counted from the first day after the personal notification of the Resolution. If the tenth day is a non-working day, the term is automatically extended to the next working day. This term is peremptory and cannot be extended.

849. Failure to appeal in due time eliminates the opportunity of seeking the annulment of the Resolution before the Contentious Administrative Court, which is a jurisdictional or contentious venue.

850. When administrative appeals are submitted in time, the administration may do one of the following: (i) revoke the challenged resolution; (ii) partially revoke it; or (iii) fail to decide on the administrative appeals.

851. When the resolution is revoked as suggested in the administrative appeals, there is no harm caused to the appealing party.

852. However, the other party or parties involved which were comfortable with the revoked resolution may be entitled to seek the annulment of this new resolution directly before the Contentious Administrative Court.

853. When the appealed resolution is revoked partially, the appealing party is entitled to file the annulment demand before the Contentious Administrative Court within the term of sixty days. This term is suspended during the judicial holidays.

854. If the administration fails to decide on the administrative appeals submitted against the resolution within two hundred days counted from the day on which they were submitted, these appeals will be considered to have been legally dismissed, thus enabling the appealing party to seek annulment of the Resolution before the Contentious Administrative Court. Therefore, the complaint should be submitted within the term of sixty days.

§3. Scope of Judicial Review

855. The scope of the judicial review, meaning the amplitude of the review, entails only an analysis of the *legality* of the Authority's decision. The Court is not allowed to re-examine the case on its merits.

856. The scope of the review can be as follows:

(1) Annulment or modification by the administration.
(2) Right to file a petition.
(3) Right to seek damages before the civil Courts.

857. (i) First, the Resolution (and any resolution) can be amended by the administration, by itself, even without the filing of any appeal. The administration does not require the filing of appeals to be able to amend the acts and adapt them to legality, if that should be the case. The only limits to this power/duty of the administration of adapting its activity to legality are those related to the stability of the act and not those affecting legal certainty.

858. (ii) In addition, the interested parties may request the revision of an administrative act by the administration, pursuant to sections 30 and 318 of the Constitution. These sections establish the right of petition; in section 30, the right of petition is granted to all individuals and in section 318, it is limited to those who have a legitimate interest in the broad sense of the word, as it includes those who hold a subjective interest.

859. Although in both cases the administration has the obligation to decide the petitions filed, only in section 318 it is anticipated that after the lapse of a certain period of time, it can be deemed that the petition has been denied, enabling the interested party to file against this denial due to the time elapsed, the administrative appeals that may correspond to section 317 of the Constitution.

860. However, neither the request for an act to be revised pursuant to section 318 of the Uruguayan Constitution, nor the denial to make such revision, or the administrative appeals against such denial reopens the opportunity to request the annulment of the original act before the Contentious Administrative Court.

861. (iii) Finally, the inability to request the annulment of the Resolution in a contentious venue does not imply, however, that the interested party cannot claim before the competent Courts for any eventual damage that the resolution may have caused. In such a case, the examination of the legality of the Resolution would be allowed, though without being able to annul it.

862. As per section 312 of the Constitution (in the wording it contains since the constitutional amendment of 1997), those who consider themselves to have been harmed by an administrative act need not obtain the annulment of such act before the Supreme Administrative Court in order to be entitled to request the repair for the damage caused.

863. In this particular case, this means that the opportunity to file a claim against the government for the damage that the Resolution may have caused or still causes exists, even if the possibility of obtaining the annulment of the Resolution in a contentious venue does not exist and even without obtaining the annulment of the Resolution by the Supreme Administrative Court.

864. This claim for damages should be filed before the competent Courts of the Judicial Power. In this respect, it must be mentioned, however, that some of the Civil Courts of Appeal resolving claims for damages filed against the government comprehend that it is not admissible to claim damages when the administrative venue has not been exhausted, that is, that a claim for damages caused by an administrative act cannot be filed when the corresponding administrative appeals were not filed against such act.

865. This judicial opinion comprehends that the omission in filing the administrative appeals is equivalent to the consent of the act. This is not the majority opinion, and the authors understand that this is not a correct interpretation of the law, but it should be taken into account anyway.

Selected Bibliography

Andrew I. Gavil, William E. Kovacic & Jonathan B. Baker. *Antitrust Law in Perspective: Cases, Concepts and Problems in Competition Policy*. Thomson-West, 2002.

Berná y otros, Leonardo. *Historia Económica del Uruguay*. Monteverde, Montevideo 2009.

Berdaguer, Jaime. Control de la Concentración Empresarial. Estudios Sobre Defensa De La Competencia Y Relaciones De Consumo. FCU, Montevideo, 2008.

Benjamín Nahum. Breve Historia del Uruguay Independiente. Banda Oriental, Montevideo, 2011.

Black's Law Dictionary. *Eight Edition* (2004).

Cage, Alan. el Ciclo Económico. *Breve historia económica del Uruguay.*

Charles de Secondat, Baron de la Brede et de Montesquieu. *de L'Espiritu Des Lois, Chapter VI, Book XI, ediciones Altaya S.A., Barcelona* (1996).

Camilo Martínez Blanco. *Grandes cadenas, poder dominante y defensa de la competencia.* FCU (2001).

Camilo Martínez Blanco. *Manual Básico de Derecho de la Competencia.* FCU (2008).

Diego Galante. *Operaciones de Adquisiciones y Fusiones en la Nueva Legislación de Competencia, CADE 21/08/2007.*

European Union Report. European Commission. *Re: Mercosur. Regional Strategy Paper–2007-2013. 02.08.2007. (2/2007/1640).*

García, Ricardo Olivera. *Introducción al derecho de la competencia. Nuevo Régimen de Derecho de la Competencia. Um* (2001).

Guillermo Cabanellas de las Cuevas. *Derecho antimonopólico y defensa de la competencia – editorial ELIASTA S.R.L. Buenos Aires* (1983).

Gerardo Caffera. *el Negocio Jurídico y la Legislación Nacional de Defensa de la Competencia ('Antitrust'). Anuario de derecho civil uruguayo, tomo XXI.*

Gary Duval & Nadine Mendal. *Knowledgeable Franchisee Exemptions Law and Policy, Federal Trade Commission E-magazine* (2005).

Gregory J. Sidak. 'Abolishing the Price Squeeze as a Theory of Antitrust Liability'. *Journal of Competition Law and Economics* 4, no. 2 (2008).

Julio Cesar Porteiro. *Evaluación de Proyectos de Inversión. Perspectiva Empresarial.* FCU, Montevideo, 2003.

John C. Coffee, Jr. '*No Soul to Damn; No Body to Kick*: An Unscandalized Inquiry into the Problem of Corporate Punishment', *Michigan Law Review*(1981): 386.

Selected Bibliography

Jaime Berdaguer. *Control de la Concentración Empresarial, Estudios sobre Defensa de la Competencia y Relaciones de Consumo.* FCU, Montevideo (2008).

Jose Tavares de Araujo Jr. *Conference on 'Competition Policy in Infrastructure Services: Second General Issues in the Reform of Public Services' Organized by the Infrastructure and Financial Markets Division and the Multilateral Investment Fundo f the Inter-American Development Bank.* Washington, D.C., 23–24 April 2001.

Kathleen F. Brickey. 'Rethinking Corporate Liability Under the Model Penal Code'. *Rutgers Law Journal* 19 (1988).

Marcelo Amorin. *Abuso de Posición Dominante e Imposición de Precios, Estudios Sobre Defensa de la Competencia y Relaciones de Consumo.* FCU, Montevideo, 2008.

Mohan Gopalan. *Corporate Criminal Sanctions*: Alternatives for the Fine City (2007).

Marcelo Carlos Quaglia. Grupos de Empresas, defensa de la Competencia y Derechos del Consumidor. La Ley, Buenos Aires (2002).

Nuri Rodríguez. *Manual de Derecho Comercial Uruguayo.*

Ortiz Blanco, Luis, Maillo González-Orus, Jerónimo; Ibáñez Colomo, Pablo y Lamadrid de Pablo, Alfonso. *Manual de derecho de la competencia.*

Osvaldo Marzorati. *Franchising*: *Astrea – Buenos Aires* (2001).

Paula Algorta Morales. *Prácticas Prohibidas. Estudios sobre defensa de la competencia y relaciones de consumo.* FCU, Montevideo (2008).

Pedro Barrán. *Historia Uruguaya.* Banda Oriental, Montevideo, 2004.

Ricardo Olivera García. *Introducción al derecho de la competencia. Nuevo Régimen de Derecho de la Competencia. Um* (2001).

Steven C. Salop. 'The First Principles Approach to Antitrust, Kodak, and Antitrust at the Millennium'. *Antitrust Law Journal* 68 (2000): 187.

Steven Nelson. Negotiating and Drafting Agency, Distribution and Franchise Agreements: American Bar Association – Section of International Law and Practice (1992).

Santiago Martínez Lage & Amadeo Petibó Juan. *Remedios y Sanciones en el Derecho de la Competencia.* Marcial Pons, Madrid (2008).

Thomas C. Arthur. *SMU Law Review* 62 (2009).

U.S. Department of Justice and the Federal Trade Commission. *Horizontal Merger Guidelines (revised 1997).*

Wayner Lafave. *Substantive Criminal Law* 2 (2003).

Index

The numbers here refer to paragraph numbers.

Made in the USA
Monee, IL
18 October 2026

66041419R10085